Launching Enterprise Products

How to Navigate Strategy, Influence, and Delivery in Complex Organizations

Anusha Ravi
Nitika Malhotra

AF719359

Apress®

Launching Enterprise Products: How to Navigate Strategy, Influence, and Delivery in Complex Organizations

Anusha Ravi
Frisco, Texas, USA

Nitika Malhotra
Sunnyvale, California, USA

ISBN-13 (pbk): 979-8-8688-2660-3
ISBN-13 (electronic): 979-8-8688-2661-0
https://doi.org/10.1007/979-8-8688-2661-0

Copyright © 2026 by Anusha Ravi and Nitika Malhotra

This work is subject to copyright. All rights are reserved by the Publisher, whether the whole or part of the material is concerned, specifically the rights of translation, reprinting, reuse of illustrations, recitation, broadcasting, reproduction on microfilms or in any other physical way, and transmission or information storage and retrieval, electronic adaptation, computer software, or by similar or dissimilar methodology now known or hereafter developed.

Trademarked names, logos, and images may appear in this book. Rather than use a trademark symbol with every occurrence of a trademarked name, logo, or image we use the names, logos, and images only in an editorial fashion and to the benefit of the trademark owner, with no intention of infringement of the trademark.

The use in this publication of trade names, trademarks, service marks, and similar terms, even if they are not identified as such, is not to be taken as an expression of opinion as to whether or not they are subject to proprietary rights.

While the advice and information in this book are believed to be true and accurate at the date of publication, neither the authors nor the editors nor the publisher can accept any legal responsibility for any errors or omissions that may be made. The publisher makes no warranty, express or implied, with respect to the material contained herein.

Managing Director, Apress Media LLC: Welmoed Spahr
Acquisitions Editor: Aditee Mirashi
Editorial Assistant: Rachel Zhang

Cover designed by eStudioCalamar

Cover image designed by Pexels

Distributed to the book trade worldwide by Springer Science+Business Media New York, 1 New York Plaza, New York, NY 10004. Phone 1-800-SPRINGER, fax (201) 348-4505, e-mail orders-ny@springer-sbm.com, or visit www.springeronline.com. Apress Media, LLC is a Delaware LLC and the sole member (owner) is Springer Science + Business Media Finance Inc (SSBM Finance Inc). SSBM Finance Inc is a **Delaware** corporation.

For information on translations, please e-mail booktranslations@springernature.com; for reprint, paperback, or audio rights, please e-mail bookpermissions@springernature.com.

Apress titles may be purchased in bulk for academic, corporate, or promotional use. eBook versions and licenses are also available for most titles. For more information, reference our Print and eBook Bulk Sales web page at http://www.apress.com/bulk-sales.

Any source code or other supplementary material referenced by the author in this book is available to readers on GitHub. For more detailed information, please visit https://www.apress.com/gp/services/source-code.

If disposing of this product, please recycle the paper

Table of Contents

About the Authors

Anusha Ravi is a senior product leader with over a decade of experience launching enterprise products from 0 to 1. She has led platform and customer systems work at companies like Intuit, Walmart, Microsoft, and Tango Analytics—often operating at the messy intersection of user needs, tech complexity, and organizational change. Her work has shaped how large teams collect insights, build with clarity, and scale with purpose. This book is deeply personal—it brings together playbooks, patterns, and lessons she's used (and battle-tested) over the years to build products that actually ship and stick. Outside of work, Anusha mentors emerging talent, judges startup competitions, and loves helping others find their voice in product leadership.

Nitika Malhotra is a product leader with 7+ years of experience building 0 to 1 and growth products across enterprise and marketplace environments. Across Walmart and Tango Analytics, she has built and scaled products in complex, cross-functional ecosystems where incentives, systems, and execution all have to line up. She is known for navigating gray spaces, filling in what is missing, and acting as a catalyst to move complex work forward. Her strengths span product strategy and execution, driving stakeholder alignment across product, engineering, and go-to-market partners, and translating technical constraints into customer-ready outcomes. This book distills what she has learned while shipping through that reality, including how to make decisions, build alignment, and scale products that actually work.

About the Technical Reviewer

Saaniya Chugh is a senior technology consultant with over a decade of experience in IT service management, enterprise automation, and ServiceNow platform implementations. She has led large-scale digital transformation initiatives across a range of clients and industries specializing in AI-driven solutions, IT governance, and workflow optimization. Based in Canada, Saaniya works at the forefront of intelligent IT systems, advising clients on the effective implementation of the ServiceNow platform.

A recognized thought leader in the ServiceNow ecosystem, she regularly contributes to industry forums and supports the ServiceNow community. She has been recognized at multiple platforms for her expertise and continues to influence the evolution of modern IT operations and enterprise service platforms.

Acknowledgments

This book was built the same way most enterprise products are built: with imperfect information, too many stakeholders, and a suspicious number of meetings.

Thank you to the mentors who gave us the kind of feedback that stings a little and makes you better. Thank you to our engineering, design, and data partners for tolerating ambiguity, translating reality, and shipping despite it. Thank you to the customer-facing teams for keeping us honest and to the users who told us what they actually needed, not just what sounded good in a roadmap review.

To our families and friends: thank you for letting this book borrow our weekends, our evenings, and our brain space. Your support made the difference more than you know.

And to you, reader: thanks for choosing the chaos. We hope these pages save you a few cycles, a few scars, and at least one unnecessary dashboard.

Introduction

The 0→1 Enterprise Challenge

Imagine this—You are introducing yourself as the product manager for one of the MAANG companies in your friends group. The moment you say you're a product manager, the mental image people get is highly romanticized. Uber cool, tech savvy, enterprising, "CEO of your product" building sleek stuff, collaborating, synergizing (ugh), managing stakeholders, and charming. You are practically "the" person making your product run. You are everything. You command energy in high-stakes rooms. It just sounds like the dream job. Satisfying and commercial at the same time. And let's not forget the money! You make the big bucks.

Ok, ok, enough dreaming. Wake up.

Let's be honest—launching new products, especially in Enterprise or at scale, is not romantic at all. It's not for the faint of heart. Everything that is romanticized is the tip of the iceberg. It is what it could look like on the outside after a mind-numbing number of hours in meetings, making decisions, convincing stakeholders, taking risks, vetting your data, and above all, staying organized and focused.

Let's be honest. You are not Steve Jobs or Bill Gates. You're not in a startup garage chasing a clean idea with a clean team. When you are in Enterprise, you are often working with a large organization with many established processes. Established processes = Established expectations. And you cannot afford to fail. You're navigating stakeholder landmines, partial buy-in, and data that's either missing or misaligned. You're building in a system that's already moving—with its own constraints, timelines, drama, and office politics. And usually, by the time a problem hits your desk, it's already gone through six layers of translation and two decks. That's the real 0→1.

But you know that—You already know all this. That's why you are here. This book is for people like you, who choose to build in that environment. For the chaos wranglers, for the eternal optimist, for the never-say-nevers. Over the last few years, we have built products from scratch within Enterprise orgs, where you have to navigate chaos. We have also established platforms, analytics, testing pipelines, customer insight systems, new business opportunities, whitespace expansion, and tools that didn't exist but were needed. We have done it with lean teams, half-roadmaps, and more than one sideways OKR (Objectives and Key Results).

This book is not a template or a framework. This book is rooted in reality. This book offers a unique blend of a looking glass into enterprise product building, combined with some dry humor and some excellent lessons learned from our own journeys so far. Our goal is to inspire the next generation of PMs to continue building enterprise products, persist through tough times, and provide a cheat sheet of some tricks of the trade. A mentor once said, "Product management isn't something you learn once. It's an apprenticeship trade—shaped by lived experiences, the mistakes and breakthroughs of others, and the collective wisdom we share as a community." We hope this book will serve as just that for you!

CHAPTER 1

Finding the Problem Behind the Brief

The first step in the product lifecycle is identifying the right problem or whitespace: clearly defining the problem statement.

Often, it begins like this: "Hey, can we build a self-serve portal for X?" or "We need to launch X by year-end." There's no context, just a vague idea that grows into a problem. Enterprise PMs typically join at this stage, usually after strategic business alignment. Welcome to product inception in enterprise. Not exactly the dream, is it?

In enterprise, it starts with organizational complexity. PMs must decode signals from noise, work within existing systems, and solve presented problems without disrupting what already works. The first challenge isn't what to build, but *why* the problem exists—and whether addressing it delivers real value to both the business and customers.

Now, let's break down how to approach this stage.

Start with Framing the Problem

You get hired or onboarded to a new product ask. Typically, the ask even comes with a prescriptive solution. If you are one of the lucky ones, you probably get just the problem statement. Welcome to enterprise!

Spoiler Alert: The first ask is never the real ask.

Don't react to surface requests. Pull the thread by asking: Who's asking? Why? How often? What are they truly trying to achieve? What if it's not done?

Let's play it with an example:

The "We Need a Dashboard" Request

Surface ask:

© Anusha Ravi and Nitika Malhotra 2026
A. Ravi and N. Malhotra, *Launching Enterprise Products*, https://doi.org/10.1007/979-8-8688-2661-0_1

The sales leadership team comes to Product with urgency: "We need a real-time sales dashboard showing every metric across all regions. Can we get this built in the next quarter? We've even sketched the layout."

Why it *looks* urgent:

A senior executive brings a "solution" and mockup as urgent and critical for decisions. Early PMs often take these as marching orders and move to execution.

Pause. Dig deeper—start with: Who's asking? Regional sales VP for field managers.

Also think—Why are they asking? They want visibility into missed targets and pipeline risk. They request custom reports from analytics several times per month. They want to spot underperforming territories early for quick action. Without it, insight and action are delayed, resulting in missed revenue.

Reframed problem:

When you look at it this way, you will realize the ask is not about a flashy dashboard at all—it's about real-time territory performance monitoring and reducing lag between data and action.

So how can you go about solving it? Instead of building the exact mockup, partner with Analytics to:

1. Automate alerts for the three most critical sales KPIs.
2. Flag KPI patterns signaling issues early. Gather dashboard feedback to confirm accuracy.
3. Provide drill-down capability in the existing BI tool instead of a separate custom build.

This in turn can result in reduced ad hoc report requests by 80%, improved underperforming territory detection in real time, and save hours and hours of data analysis and cleanup labor.

And most of all, you solved the pain point behind the ask, rather than just blindly delivering what was asked for as is. Once you pull the thread, half your job early on is being the translator. You're turning vague business-speak into real product thinking. And sometimes that means digging five layers deep before you even find a problem worth solving. This is what you may have heard of in the 5W's framework.

Get your hands dirty. Think—*is there a market for this, and will it be disruptive or additive?* Sometimes you go additive and sometimes you disrupt, but there has to be a balance. You can't continuously add without disrupting—then you're just one more face in the crowd. But if you only disrupt, you're just creating chaos. You need the grit and the discipline to do both.

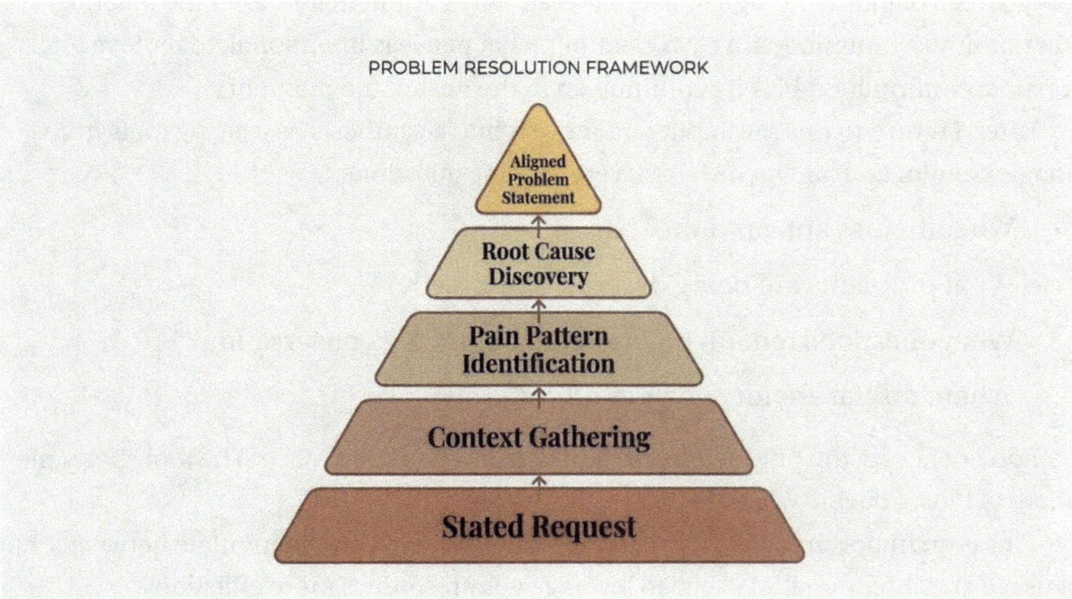

Figure 1-1. *Problem Resolution Framework*

How can you leverage AI to do this faster and smarter

In enterprise discovery, clarity rarely arrives at the moment someone finishes a sentence. It arrives later—after multiple conversations, contradictions, and half-formed ideas collide. To handle this, I do not rely on memory or post-meeting summaries. I rely on a live, thinking workspace.

During stakeholder meetings, I open a running thread on NotebookLM or Notion—and type continuously as the meeting unfolds. This is not structured note-taking. It is a raw dump of consciousness.

What goes in:

- Exact phrases stakeholders use (especially emotionally loaded ones)
- My internal reactions ("this sounds like a proxy problem," "this contradicts last week")

- Questions I choose not to ask yet
- Potential pivots or reframes
- Moments where energy spikes or drops in the room

I do this without formatting, bullets, or cleanup. Speed matters more than polish. The goal is to capture the signal before it evaporates. Immediately after the meeting, I do nothing. No summarizing. No cleaning. That pause is intentional, to remove any personal confirmation bias if I continue on in the heat of the moment.

Later, I return to this raw input and move it into a synthesis pass using tools from Google Gemini and/or OpenAI. I ask very specific questions:

"What themes appear more than once?"

"What problems are being described indirectly?"

"What questions remain unanswered across the conversation?"

"Where do stakeholder goals conflict?"

I do not accept the output as truth. I treat it as a pattern surface. The tool shows me where to look. I decide what matters.

This is an important tactic for working smart—where you differentiate between blind AI usage and intentional AI usage to leverage your resources more efficiently.

Pattern Behind the Pain

Let's go deeper. How do you understand the 5W's?

- **WHAT** is broken today (observable friction, not a missing feature)
- **WHO** feels the pain most (primary pain holders vs. adjacent stakeholders)
- **WHY** the problem exists (root cause, not surface symptoms)
- **WHY NOW** (what changed, scaled, or crossed a breaking point)
- **WHAT is the cost of inaction** (operational, behavioral, or financial)

The thing about enterprise product building? Everything is noisy. Everything is a need. Every team has their "top pain point." Every leader has a different interpretation of the north star, the Objectives and Key Results (OKRs) don't align, and every group is chasing a slightly varied north star. Every customer account thinks their use case is the most important.

And your job as the PM. To make sense of this chaos. So how do you prioritize?

You zoom out.

You look for themes that repeat across roles and functions.

Focus on recurring patterns, not just anecdotes.

For example, let us consider lead generation tracking inside an enterprise. Sales kept losing deals because prospects asked: *"Does your system integrate cleanly with a CRM?"* and the answer was usually "not yet" or "sometimes"—that doesn't breed confidence. Support was flooded with tickets as customers manually exported CSVs to upload into their CRMs. Imagine doing this in the age of AI. Inside the company, five different teams had built one-off connectors and brittle scripts to make the data flow in an automated way in an attempt to help. And account management teams rebuilt shadow spreadsheets monthly to reconcile sales.

Individually, these seemed like different "asks." Collectively, they revealed the unmet need for a fully integrated CRM system covering lead generation, management, data pipelines, real-time sales, and support.

Taking stakeholders at face value could lead to a 'franken-monster' system. Instead, by listening for recurring pain, you found the real pattern. Mastering this process saves time and money and delivers a problem statement everyone supports.

How does AI help in this phase?

Pattern recognition breaks down when inputs are scattered. Emails in one place. Meeting notes in another. Old decks forgotten. To counter this, I deliberately centralize discovery inputs in a single system—typically a workspace like NotebookLM/Notion/OneNote.

Each problem space gets one living page. Inside it, I maintain four explicit sections:

1. Raw Inputs (meeting notes, voice transcripts, pasted emails)
2. Recurring Themes (updated only after synthesis passes, typically by Gemini or OpenAI)
3. Unresolved Questions (things that keep resurfacing)

4. Hypotheses and Pivots (explicit, even when uncomfortable, and especially when it is questioning the premise)

Every few days, I run a consolidation pass using language models. I paste the latest raw inputs as well as provide access to recurring themes, unresolved questions, and hypotheses and ask:

- "Update the recurring themes section."
- "List unresolved but repeating concerns."
- "Identify assumptions stated as facts."

This is how vague enterprise chaos turns into visible structure. Patterns stop living in your head and start living on the page—where they can be challenged, refined, and defended.

And that becomes your superpower. You become the PM who is on top of their game, top of their research, and top of their stakeholders. You become the grandmaster in this game of chess.

Avoid the Mine

Say it loud with me: problem briefs > product briefs. One of my leaders used to say—*love the problem, not the product.*

But the motivational reward system is inverted. Product managers get typically rewarded for shipping. But if we ship a bad product, nothing is more painful than cleaning up that mess. It's almost like playing a game of Minesweeper. If you make the right moves, great. But if you hit a mine, then it's going to take a while to get back on track.

To avoid mines, start by framing the problem well. Features usually fail not from poor construction, but from solving the wrong problem or the right one in the wrong context.

Before writing any Product Requirement Documents (PRD), get clear on the 5W's—**What's broken or inefficient today? Who's feeling the pain and how? What is the job to be done? Why now? What's the cost of inaction?**

For example, how many times have we heard this recurring need to have a dashboard that summarizes all the information. And dashboards sell. It's flashy, it gets the sound bytes, and it's easy to consume. Dashboards make numbers look authentic.

It's almost like your data and metrics got put into a fancy tuxedo. Everyone loves it and what not. It just felt like the right thing. Almost too obvious. But is that the answer? Well, let's see about that.

When you break it down into these five questions above, the problem crystallizes further. Let us put our 5W's in action here.

What's broken or inefficient today? The information summarization and synthesization process of getting to the key insights. Simply said—what is the story behind the numbers? **Who's feeling the pain and how?** Customers are feeling the pain because they have to go through Excel gymnastics to get to the answer. **What is the job to be done?** Get the top 3 recurring questions to be answered to be always present and sticky on the dashboard. **What is the cost of inaction?** The process is broken, and the longer it stays broken, the larger the cost. **Why now?** The longer that we take to act on this, the more users are having to adapt to a highly manual process, causing friction, retention issues, and a higher level of customer complaints.

This clarifies the real problem: The need isn't necessarily a dashboard itself, but automated, actionable answers to the top three recurring business questions so users get timely insights without manual effort. Now ultimately in this case, if a dashboard is the easiest way to surface that, sure, why not? The point being, don't jump to the three-piece tux as the outfit for every occasion, but on some occasions, like a wedding, the three-piece tux might just be the right answer. Weigh your 5W's before deciding on the approach.

And here's a tip that's saved me more than once: write the "Why This Exists" paragraph as if you're defending the budget to a skeptical CFO. Different companies do this in different ways. Amazon has this PR FAQ model, where they position the problem as if you are defending a launch day press release. If it doesn't hold up there, it's not tight enough. And now with all the AI tools at our disposal, you can have AI be your most skeptical stakeholder and poke holes in your theory until you feel the problem is distilled.

So how do we use AI for this? Let's deep dive.

When it's time to write a problem statement, I do not start writing. I start assembling inputs.

My writing workflow is deliberately mechanical, structured, and repeatable:

Input 1: Raw notes from the discovery workspace

Input 2: Voice notes recorded immediately after key meetings (often 2–5 minutes long, unfiltered)

Input 3: My organization's standard PRD or problem template

Input 4: One short paragraph written by me answering: What problem are we solving, for whom, and why now—very rough and ready.

These inputs are fed into a drafting pass using tools like ChatGPT or Gemini with very explicit instructions:

"Do not invent content."

"Preserve uncertainty."

"Flag weak assumptions."

"Structure this using the provided template."

The output is a first draft—not a decision. I then switch back to human mode: cutting, tightening, rewriting, and pressure-testing every claim. The tool accelerates consolidation. I own the argument.

And that brings us to our next section on pressure testing.

Pressure Testing

Once you think you've got something, resist the urge to go into a doc-writing cave. Start *jamming*. Run a cross-functional idea jam. Invite people who will eventually care: customer-facing teams, engineers, ops leads, your closest friendly skeptic. Don't aim for alignment—aim for *pressure*. See what breaks. Trust me, you are going to get the most interesting edge cases and hypotheses in these jams. And an added bonus: you are already pre-aligning AND energizing your stakeholders. I know there is no such thing as a magic formula or secret sauce in product, but this one comes pretty close to one for me. This jamming and pre-aligning pretty much makes or breaks the journey.

Sketch flows. Play out edge cases. Ask people how *they* would solve it with what already exists. Then ask: What's still missing? And then listen. Listen with your eyes and ears. See what excites the stakeholder and what stresses them. If you want to go further, test the framing externally. Grab a call with a few customers. Don't pitch a feature, pitch the problem. Validate the pain point. Ask them:

"How are you solving this today? "What's annoying about that? "If this didn't exist tomorrow, what happens to your day? Or the flip side of it: "If this existed tomorrow, how much would it change your day/process?" If they shrug? You're too early. If they rant? You're probably late. If they say, "I've been trying to do that for *months*," congratulations—go build your case.

Before you can sell a solution, you have to sell the need. We will get into this more in coming chapters. This is where pressure testing your problem statement really gets going. This part often gets skipped in enterprise because people assume the stakeholder who asked already knows the value. People forget why something mattered in the first place. And priorities shift every quarter.

How can AI help?

Well, if you are the counselor, AI is your paralegal. Use AI to prep and test here.

Pressure testing is the point where friction is intentionally invited before it appears in the room. Once a working hypothesis exists, it is not immediately socialized or defended. Instead, it is subjected to multiple rounds of internal stress using tools such as ChatGPT or Gemini—not to validate the idea, but to interrogate it from angles that will inevitably surface later.

The same problem framing is restated in several different ways, sometimes sharpened, sometimes deliberately weakened, and evaluated from the perspectives of expected stakeholders: an executive sponsor scanning for strategic coherence, a skeptical engineer probing for edge cases, a legal partner assessing risk exposure, a sales leader prioritizing speed, or an operator who will live with the downstream consequences long after the meeting ends. Each pass reveals a different fault line. Assumptions that initially felt reasonable begin to show fragility. Mentally justified trade-offs expose gaps in articulation. Questions emerge that would quietly derail the conversation if left unaddressed.

From there, iteration focuses not on the solution itself, but on the framing. Logic is tightened where it is loose. Guardrails are added where the blast radius is unclear. Intent is clarified where ambiguity could be mistaken for indecision. The objective is not to make the proposal bulletproof but to make it honest.

Inevitably, some gaps remain—areas that cannot be responsibly closed without more data, more time, more discussion, or a different bet altogether. These gaps are not buried. They are surfaced explicitly as assumptions. The most uncomfortable questions are introduced early, not as weaknesses, but as known trade-offs. In high-stakes enterprise environments, surprises erode trust faster than imperfect answers.

By naming the hardest questions upfront, the dynamic shifts away from defense and toward collaboration, enabling decisions to be made with shared clarity about both the upside and the risks being consciously accepted.

Well, that's all about the problems, my friends. We have got 99 problems, but crafting a good problem statement isn't one anymore. In summary:

- Start with framing the problem
- Identify the Pattern behind the Pain
- Avoid the mine
- Pressure Test, Pressure Test, Pressure Test!

You're not here to react. You're here to make sense of the chaos. Remember you are the chaos wrangler. And spot the opportunity hiding behind the noise. And then you are here to work the problem, work the room, work the stakeholders, work the market, and ultimately work up your success. Bored of the amount of work that we have to work on? Well, my friend, *that's* the real work of 0→1. Welcome on board!

CHAPTER 2

Bringing People In (Without Losing the Wheel)

You've found the problem. You have framed it clearly. Maybe even sparked a little buzz and built some excitement during the pressure testing. Now comes the real challenge—**bringing people in without letting them take over**. How often do you go with a super clear problem statement and a picture-perfect vision and suddenly find yourself lost by the time week 4 rolls in.

You've probably faced this at work or even just planning a group dinner or a friend trip. Once you bring people in, everyone's got a point of view. And once the door is open, they'll walk in with their own roadmap opinions, their own metrics, and their own reasons why this thing should be bigger/smaller/green/livestreamed by Tuesday. Suddenly it feels like you are on a very vocal news program. Worry not, you are exactly where you need to be. This chaos is where a true Enterprise PM thrives. You invited people in because you wanted varying perspectives. You want to understand the problem from all sides. But you want to still hold the room. You want to listen, but not get steamrolled. Think of yourself as the coach of a football team. You need to hold space for all the chaos, all the perspectives, but remember you ultimately have to motivate everyone and make everyone work toward a common goal.

The trick as a PM is how do you listen to the committee and gain from the perspectives while also maintaining the true north to the problem statement? So let's talk about how to collaborate *without giving up ownership*. How to get alignment *by consensus*. And how to harness *stakeholders as accelerants, not anchors.*

Now as you are reading this, you may think, "Well, easier said than done." Agreed! However, here are a few battle-tested approaches that you can take.

© Anusha Ravi and Nitika Malhotra 2026
A. Ravi and N. Malhotra, *Launching Enterprise Products*, https://doi.org/10.1007/979-8-8688-2661-0_2

Forget the Title and Know Your Power

You do not need to be the most senior person in the room to lead. But you do need to own the room like the one who's done the homework. You need to be Hermoine Granger from Harry Potter. People will follow the person who owns the problem, understands the stakes, and makes the path forward clearer. That's your edge.

Remember your problem statement before you start your preparation. That is your north star. Great, now let's prepare for that homework. Here are a few things that we can do to set ourselves up for success.

Clarify the goal of the meeting

Every meeting must have one: are we validating a direction, allocating resources, or sequencing milestones? Write it down in one sentence at the top. Have this in the meeting invite as the subject. Repeat it multiple times as you kick off the meeting. There should be no ambiguity to the participants about what the goal of the meeting is. This sets a clean pathway for everyone to move in a cohesive direction toward a common goal.

Alignment rarely fails because people lack information. It fails because people experience conversations differently and leave with different interpretations of what just happened. In enterprise environments, this divergence begins the moment a meeting ends.

How can AI help here?

To reduce this drift, meetings are treated not as events but as inputs into a shared thinking system. Conversations are captured using tools such as Zoom note-taking and transcription, not for recordkeeping, but for synthesis. Raw transcripts are never circulated as-is. Instead, they are processed immediately into structured artifacts that answer three questions: what was decided, what remains open, and what assumptions surfaced implicitly. Over time you can train this into a template as well.

This approach shifts meetings away from memory contests and toward shared clarity. When the same interpretation is available to everyone, alignment becomes something that can be inspected and corrected, rather than assumed.

Define the boundaries

Know what's already off the table (e.g., scope, timelines, or budget). This prevents idea sprawl and keeps focus on feasible solutions. And if the boundaries get pushed, gently remind the group of the goal and assert the goal. Fellow parents may understand that this is very much akin to gently redirecting a toddler without setting the stage for a full-blown meltdown.

Anticipate friction

List your top three expected pushbacks. You want them; you need them. This is usually where you will make or break the case. But how can you successfully do so? By having clean data that is summarized, use insights or trade-off tables to ground opinions in evidence.

How can AI help here?

Early stakeholder conversations generate more signal than any formal document, but only if that signal is captured and consolidated before it fragments. To enable this, stakeholder inputs are centralized in a single workspace, most often using systems like Notion. Each initiative is given a living page that evolves alongside the work.

This page does not summarize opinions. It organizes them. Typical sections include:

- Stakeholder perspectives (verbatim where useful)
- Areas of agreement
- Areas of tension
- Unresolved questions
- Assumptions driving positions

Inputs from meetings, transcripts, and written feedback are periodically synthesized using language models from OpenAI or Google. The objective is not consensus, but visibility. When disagreement is visible and explicit, it becomes something that can be addressed rather than quietly worked around. This also

Visualize alignment

Don't let discussion float in abstraction. Use frameworks like a decision-making canvas like Figma, Mural, or Miro Virtually or a whiteboard in person and have an organized layout of information hierarchy that you want to discuss to lead you from Point A to Point B.

Let's play this out. Say you're a mid-level PM leading a new **AI-based workflow automation feature**. It's a cross-team initiative—data science, design, and engineering all have opinions; customer success has anecdotes; and sales wants it yesterday. You're not the most senior person in the room, but you *are* the one connecting all the dots.

Here is how you can take the wheel. Map out potential rollout options in a shared board or document—but don't hardline on any idea. Think of this like providing three possible doors that you have already pre-vetted and are confident that they are feasible, and now you are working with all stakeholders to decide which route to go.

You've pre-tagged each stakeholder in a RACI section: who's a reviewer, who's an approver, and who's merely informed. This helps everyone center on their role when the meeting starts to get chaotic. You've sent out a preread the day before, with the question clearly stated—"Do we prioritize accuracy or automation speed in the first release?"

Now, despite all this preparation, when in the meeting, let's assume the conversation starts spiraling:

Data Science wants to maximize accuracy. Engineering warns about model drift. Sales insists customers don't care about accuracy if the feature is slow. This is your time to take the wheel once again. You bring everyone back to the *problem statement—* Clarifying the Goal: "Our goal is to reduce customer time-to-completion by 30% while maintaining baseline trust levels." You show a simple chart comparing tradeoffs between speed and accuracy (thanks to anticipated friction points) and then summarize stakeholder inputs visually on the board. Within 20 minutes, the debate turns into a decision. The team agrees to roll out a **"Speed-First Beta"** with accuracy thresholds monitored via telemetry, and you assign next steps to each function.

A couple of key things to note here is as an enterprise PM, you have to be fast on your feet—you need to listen while anticipating the next move and having simple charts and visuals done quickly while you are enabling the conversation. And you have to be persistent—you have to prepare the preread and have options laid out while simultaneously expecting your stakeholders to come unprepared or already biased to an option. You have to be willing to repeat yourself and bring the room back to focus when they go on a random tangent. No one appointed you the decider and the aggregator—but you became the gravitational center because you defined the decision, structured the dialog, translated opinion into evidence, and guided the team to closure.

That's power without title—and that's what enterprise leadership often looks like.

Edit Ruthlessly

How do you wield this power and influence as a PM, and how do you connect with your audience effectively and drive decisions? This is where a critical skill comes in.

Bringing people in too late creates blockers. Bringing them in too early dilutes focus. Your job is to curate inclusion—to invite diversity of thought without surrendering direction. Think of yourself as akin to a famous fashion designer. You start with a lot, and then you edit, edit, edit till it's sculpted to perfection.

Early in a 0→1 cycle, collaboration is essential, but chaos is not. First on the list—Who to Invite (and When)—This is a lived experience and varies from organization to organization. But here is a rough checklist that has typically worked well for us.

Users first, legal next. Users reveal the truth that data alone can't. Talk to them before you polish your pitch deck or prereads—this grounds your questions, approach, and decisions in data. Once you have that, you may want legal vetting to ensure that you are on the clear from a legal standpoint before you spend time and effort. Then go to your partner who will call out magical thinking and save you three sprints of re-architecture. Your partner(s) in crime. The most fundamental building blocks of a product. Your core team leads. Next come your skeptical allies. The few who poke holes early so the steering committee doesn't do it later. Preferably the ones who like to play your devil's advocate but are still someone who understands your perspective and does not undermine it.

Also, it is typically best to bring these stakeholders one by one versus all together in the same meeting. Avoid the trap of the "Town-Hall Brainstorm." The bigger the group, the smaller the outcome. Curate your collaborators the way an editor curates contributors.

Let's play it with an example. You're designing a performance analytics dashboard. This could go one of two ways.

Week 1: ten stakeholders join your kickoff call—design, data science, sales, ops, marketing. By week 3: half the group wants new filters, one wants a live ticker, and another wants it in PowerPoint. You're now managing feedback debt, not building value. Sound familiar? Kid me not—we have all done this at least once in our enterprise product career, if not more. But these chaos points are our learning and inflection points that help us grow into a more prepared product warrior. *Contrast that with the curated approach:* Talked to three end-users to map daily friction and then cleared out your problem statement and broad approach with legal. Reviewed feasibility with your design and engineering lead and tested the hypothesis with one skeptical partner from ops. The result? A prototype everyone could align behind, because it was grounded, not bloated.

If a meeting has more than seven participants, you're not deciding—you're performing. Split ideation from decision-making. Use Miro/FigJam boards for asynchronous contribution; reserve live time for closure and only bring the leads. And when I mean leads, not the leads by title, but the lead of the initiative—the one who will ultimately design it/build it/sell it/defend it.

Alignment ≠ Agreement

Many PMs equate alignment with universal harmony. That's not alignment—that's consensus theater. And there is nothing worse than consensus theater. Trust me, this was the hardest growth point for me as I picked up the skills of the trade. I thought if everyone was happy and no one visibly disagreed, we had a consensus, and that means we are aligned. Boy, have I been wrong. Sometimes consensus can lead you into a false sense of security that may tide you over till you build, but the crash from that peak when you start receiving customer feedback is just brutal.

Alignment means: Everyone understands the direction. Everyone acknowledges the trade-offs. Everyone commits not to block once the decision is made. You're not aiming for group therapy; you're aiming for forward motion.

How can AI help?

Modern tooling does not replace the PM's responsibility for alignment, but it changes how that responsibility is exercised. Instead of re-explaining the same context repeatedly, alignment artifacts are reused and refined. A single source of truth is allowed to mature as understanding deepens.

Draft narratives, decision summaries, and trade-off explanations are iterated asynchronously. Early versions are intentionally rough, designed to invite correction rather than approval. Feedback is consolidated, patterns are identified, and contradictions are surfaced explicitly. This creates a feedback loop where alignment improves through iteration instead of persuasion.

Asynchronous alignment is not about efficiency. It is about reducing distortion. When people engage with the same artifact in their own time, reactions become more thoughtful and less performative. Commitment does not come from agreement alone. It comes from people seeing their concerns reflected accurately in the final framing. To support this, decision summaries explicitly call out what was accepted, what was deferred, and what trade-offs remain.

These summaries are not polished presentations. They are working documents that evolve as understanding sharpens. Over time, they become a decision history that explains not just what was done but why it made sense at the time. In complex organizations, this history is often the difference between sustained alignment and quiet erosion.

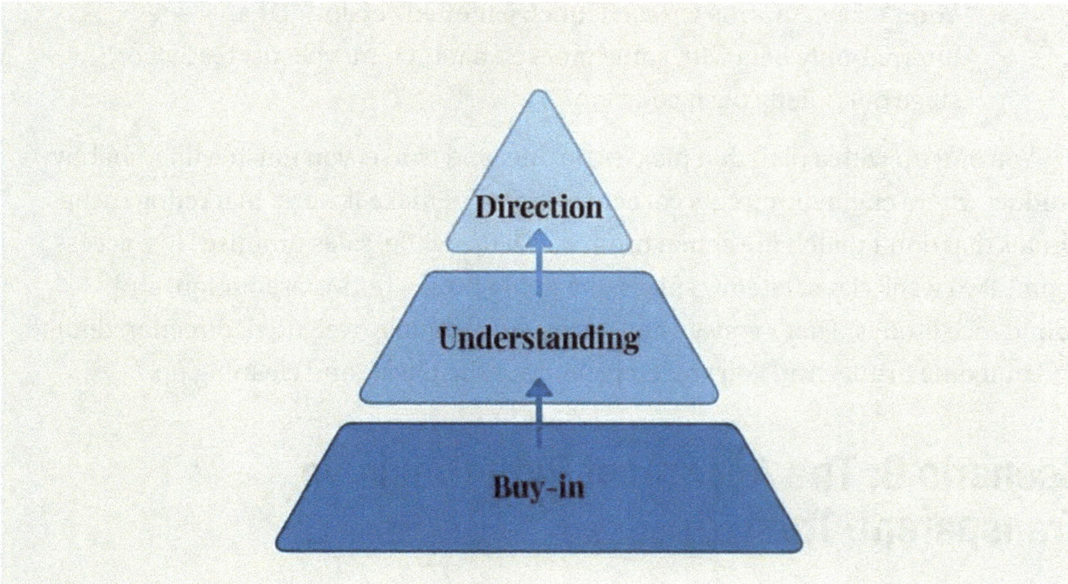

Figure 2-1. *Alignment Pyramid*

You start by setting direction, build shared understanding with transparent trade-offs, and close with buy-in—agreement to move, not to agree.

Let's say you're leading a partner integration for an enterprise platform. Engineering worries about latency. Sales is pushing for a flashy launch at the upcoming industry conference. Marketing wants polished demos. Everyone has a valid point—and a deadline.

Scenario A: The Consensus Path (a.k.a. The Compromise Spiral)

You try to make everyone happy. The meeting goes like this:

- **Sales:** "We have to announce at the conference. It's our biggest visibility play."
- **Engineering:** "The system won't hold under load yet. We need another sprint."
- **Marketing:** "If we announce, we need visuals, not a half-baked demo."

- **You:** "Okay... maybe we can launch a limited version? Or an internal-only beta with some mocked data? Or maybe just tease it on stage but quietly push code too?"

You end up with a plan that pleases no one, and worse, you finish with a shabby product where engineering cuts corners to "mostly" make it work. Marketing rushes visuals that don't match the actual product. All the while, sales promise "live access soon." Two weeks later, latency spikes, the demo breaks mid-presentation, and confidence erodes. That's consensus—every voice equally weighted, direction diluted, and outcome brittle. And you are left picking up the pieces and cleaning up.

Scenario B: The Alignment Path (Decisive, Transparent, Trusted)

You approach the same debate differently—anchored in clarity and trade-offs. You map the options visually:

Option	Benefit	Risk	Owner
Ship now	Meet PR date	10% reliability dip	Engineering
Delay 1 sprint	Stability ↑	Missed announcement window	PM + marketing

Then you summarize: "If we ship now, we gain visibility but risk trust. If we delay just by a sprint or two, we preserve quality but miss momentum. What's our optimization goal—speed or reliability? The room goes quiet. The CTO nods: "Let's soft-launch with a small set of trusted customers, collect metrics, and go public next cycle." Marketing reframes the narrative: "Coming soon—already in use by select partners." Sales still gets a talking point; engineering gets breathing room. No one got 100% of what they wanted. But everyone understood the why behind the decision—and committed not to block. That's alignment.

Lessons Learned from This

Factor	Consensus Outcome	Alignment Outcome
Decision speed	Slow, circular	Clear, time-bound
Stakeholder emotion	Temporary comfort	Informed commitment
Product quality	Compromised	Protected
PM perception	Pleaser	Leader

In Summary

- Forget the title and know your power
- Edit like you are a designer in Paris Fashion Week
- Don't confuse agreement with alignment

You're not just building a roadmap—you're building momentum, and momentum is fragile in enterprise. Protect it the way you protect uptime—because both decide whether your product actually ships.

CHAPTER 3

Scoping the First Build (Without Losing the Plot)

So what have we done so far? We have defined the problem very clearly, and we have gotten the stakeholders excited and engaged, too. So, that's it. You are in the clear. Let's go build. Well—almost, but not quite. Any product building is like playing Russian roulette. You could have defined an obvious problem, validated it with the users, and thought it was a slam dunk. But at the time of launch, it could still be a hit or miss. Building too quickly and taking user feedback verbatim can steer you away from your north star, while being too slow lands you in analysis paralysis.

And that is the Achilles heel of PMs. Either we boil the ocean and try to do everything too fast when users aren't ready for such a change, or we do the bare minimum that is good enough but underwhelming. The sweet spot lives between ambition and pragmatism: building just enough of the right thing, in the correct order, to prove the concept *and* unlock momentum. The "and" part is critical. It's not just a proof of concept or momentum. It's both. And typically, this starts with throwaway wireframes or lightweight prototypes—quick to build, easy to test. As my design friends taught me very early on in my career, these are called low-fidelity designs or Lo-Fi designs.

Let's break down how to scope a first build that hits.

Step 1: Know What You're Proving

Everyone says you should have strong metrics. I agree, but even before metrics, one of the first things we need is a clear goal for every Lo-Fi prototype to answer a question. A fundamental question that moves the business or the decision set forward. It should solve a pain point, a problem for the customer, or make their life easier by taking some of their cumbersome tasks, also known as "Jobs to be done." As builders, our job is to make

© Anusha Ravi and Nitika Malhotra 2026
A. Ravi and N. Malhotra, *Launching Enterprise Products*, https://doi.org/10.1007/979-8-8688-2661-0_3

our customers' lives easier—not more complicated. You could even take this literally and say—if you were an architect and a builder, you would want to build a home that is functional and beautiful. Form and Function.

How can you leverage AI to help here?

At this stage, AI can be used to sharpen—not shortcut—clarity. Before a single prototype is built, early hypotheses, customer pain points, and workflow assumptions can be consolidated and pressure-tested using tools like ChatGPT or Gemini. By feeding in discovery notes, early stakeholder inputs, and draft problem statements, it becomes possible to quickly surface contradictions, hidden assumptions, and gaps in logic that are easy to miss when context is spread across conversations.

This is particularly useful when translating abstract "jobs to be done" into concrete behaviors. Instead of debating internally what users might do, scenarios can be simulated: how a small business owner might approach inventory reconciliation, how a store manager might scan for low supply, or how a finance lead might look for margin leakage. These simulated walkthroughs help ensure the first build is anchored in real workflows rather than idealized ones.

Well, that's precisely what we need for enterprise product building as well.

- Will customers actually engage with this?
- Can we deliver this within the systems we have?
- Will internal teams adopt this into their workflow?

To keep these questions grounded, AI can be used as a rehearsal environment before anything reaches a customer. Draft prototype goals and success criteria can be run through ChatGPT or Gemini with explicit instructions to respond as different personas—customers, internal operators, or skeptical stakeholders. The intent is not validation but exposure: which questions feel under-defined, which success metrics sound vague, and where the prototype risks answering the wrong problem well. This exercise often reveals that a single prototype is trying to prove too much. When that happens, the scope becomes clearer—not by shrinking ambition, but by isolating the one question that must be answered first for everything else to matter.

For example, let's assume that you are building a dashboard for businesses to view, analyze, and optimize their sales as well as manage their inventory.

The first step is to build a prototype that can answer the questions above. AI tools like Lovable and Vercel have never made it easier to create working prototypes that can be taken to customers to test for impact. There are many other tools similar to Lovable, Vercel, etc. Do your research and pick the best one for your needs.

Tools such as Lovable, Vercel, and Builder.io enable PMs to move beyond static wireframes and into interactive, testable experiences far earlier than traditional workflows allow. These platforms make it possible to simulate real data flows, clickable paths, and conditional states without full backend investment.

This matters because customers respond differently to something they can use versus something they are asked to imagine. A working prototype—no matter how rough—reveals friction, hesitation, and confusion in ways no verbal feedback ever will. Even when the backend is mocked or partially manual, the perceived value can be tested authentically.

For PMs, this changes the nature of early validation. Instead of debating requirements in the abstract, conversations shift to observable behavior: where users pause, where they backtrack, and where they instinctively click next.

Once we have that, we then try to alpha test your prototype with a subset of the customers. In this example, you want a few small business owners from different market verticals to verify, who also deal with purchasing and retail. So think of your bakeries, your paint stores, your coffee shops, your bookstores. You want your alpha group to be representative of the market for which you are trying to build the product.

Then, instead of just directly asking them the questions above, create tests and exercises that will help answer the questions experientially. Try to have them do an exercise where they are asked to identify low supply and place an order directly from the dashboard. Also, ask them to identify their sales and margins and quickly find problem areas or high-growth areas. Measure the time it takes for users to reach these solutions. That shows how efficient the system is and how confidently they are engaging with the product. Typically, once you ask the question, if you stay quiet, they will automatically talk you through how they envision this fitting into their workflow, whether their employees will find it easy, any anticipated training needs, etc.

AI can also be leveraged post-session to extract insight at scale. Recordings, transcripts, and facilitator notes from alpha tests can be consolidated and analyzed using language models to surface recurring themes, confusion points, and moments of delight. Rather than relying solely on anecdotal impressions, patterns across sessions become visible quickly—especially when testing spans multiple verticals or user types.

This helps distinguish between feedback that reflects individual preference and feedback that signals a systemic usability or value issue. The result is a tighter feedback loop and more confident scoping decisions going into the first build.

Step 2: Shrink the Surface, Not the Value

Once you have the feedback on the prototype, decide what makes the first cut and what needs more fine-tuning. Take the wins and move ahead with your first lean release while addressing the areas that need fine-tuning in a fast follow. Scoping down doesn't mean making it boring. It means making it tight, making it right, and ensuring the launch lands with a punch for your cohort.

When deciding what makes the first cut, AI-assisted synthesis can help remove emotion from prioritization. Feedback, feature requests, and stakeholder asks can be grouped and summarized to reveal which items directly support the core job being validated and which are adjacent enhancements. This makes it easier to defend why certain requests are deferred without dismissing their importance.

In practice, this often means using AI to map proposed features back to the assumption or learning they support. If a feature does not materially change what will be learned in the first release, it is a candidate for deferral—regardless of how reasonable it sounds in isolation.

When shrinking the surface area of the first build without losing value, the focus should be on strategic prioritization. Instead of trying to solve for every persona, pick the one with the highest friction. Rather than building a full integration, simulate the backend and prove the value manually. Maybe consider using prototyping tools like Lovable, Builder, etc. Similarly, instead of creating a new interface, plug into something that already exists. The crucial takeaway is to ALWAYS solve a key pain point or job that the users in your cohort want, thereby making their lives easier.

Ok, so you have tested the Lo-Fi prototypes and made the calls to update your early launch scope. What do you need next—buy in for this decision? This is the part where you'll hear "we can't launch unless we have X." Fight that. Use the principles from Chapter 2. Figure out the *core interaction* or insight you're trying to validate. Build *just enough* to make that visible and valuable. Then, build on top of it later. Reassure your stakeholders you haven't forgotten their asks—they have to wait a little longer while you chase bite-sized wins. You have to be really focused and clear on this messaging. Half the job of a good PM is being the bouncer who has to ask people to wait in line and wait for their turn to get into an amazing club or party. Also, early, punchy, and bite-sized releases make people curious. Think of it like a great movie trailer—it doesn't tell the whole story, but it gets people to show up.

This is also where lightweight prototypes become powerful storytelling tools. Instead of debating hypotheticals, stakeholders can be shown exactly what will ship—and what will not—using interactive demos built in tools like Builder or Loveable. Seeing the core interaction working often reduces anxiety more effectively than verbal reassurance ever could.

AI-assisted narratives can support this process as well. Clear, concise summaries explaining what is being validated now versus later can be drafted, refined, and reused across forums, ensuring consistency in messaging even as conversations scale.

Step 3: Sequence Like a PM, Storytell Like a Founder

Now that you've scoped the MVP, don't just hand it over like a task list. Tell the story. Oh boy, if this is not a critical step.

A good PM not just makes good decisions. Then they lay out the *why now*, *what we're learning*, and *what we'll unlock next*. They don't leave the audience guessing. So how can you do this?

Build the narrative arc and set appropriate goals

- Phase 1: Build core interaction → prove engagement
- Phase 2: Layer deeper data or automation → reduce manual work
- Phase 3: Expand personas → drive adoption

This helps you manage expectations, protect against mid-cycle scope creep, and promote alignment. It shows you're thinking in terms of bets, but you are also being measured and practical about it. And more than anything, this drives the narrative deeper in the stakeholders' minds. You informed them when building the problem, when you were gaining alignment on the problem statement, and now as you are finalizing your original build scope.

Sequencing benefits from AI when treated as a narrative exercise rather than a planning one. Draft roadmap narratives, phase goals, and learning objectives can be reviewed through the lens of different audiences—executives, delivery teams, or customer-facing partners—to identify where the story breaks down or feels unconvincing.

This allows the narrative to be refined before it is socialized broadly, reducing misinterpretation and mid-cycle churn. When the story is clear, the roadmap becomes easier to defend and harder to derail.

Not just that, tell the story with the data from your Lo-FI prototyping sessions with users. If you reinvented a flow—or introduced a brand-new one—look for key metrics like clicks reduced, total time saved, workflow efficiency improved, or complaints or customer calls reduced. These are great metrics to gut-check whether you're actually solving a real problem.

And if the metrics don't give you confidence? Pivot. You'll save time, money, and effort by not building a product that was never going to land. If it does, then proceed to develop and ship. Shipping is a milestone, not a mic drop. Your job isn't done when the thing goes live. In fact, that is when things just got started. It's done when someone uses it without you explaining it, and it has generated enough traction that someone asks, "When is the next update?"

Plan your first build with post-launch learning baked within the process, like what will you measure? Who will you talk to after 2 weeks? What "early signals" count as success? Don't just track adoption—track what *changed* because of it. And then take all the lessons learned and apply them to your fast followers and the next builds.

AI can also help interpret early signals without overreacting to noise. Early usage data, qualitative feedback, and support inputs can be synthesized to answer a more important question than raw adoption: what actually changed in user behavior because this shipped?

When signals are weak or contradictory, this synthesis helps determine whether a pivot is required or whether the solution simply needs iteration. In either case, the decision is grounded in evidence rather than instinct alone.

TL;DR: Scoping with Strategy

- Know what you are building
- Scope to value, not to size
- Tell the story of what's next—before anyone asks

The right first build sets the tone. It buys you credibility. It creates demand. And most importantly, it earns you the right to keep building.

CHAPTER 4

Getting the Signal from the Noise

You have scoped the work and shipped the first version, and you are feeling cautiously optimistic. Then the familiar pattern plays out. Slack messages roll in. Someone from sales shares feedback from a customer who barely touched the feature. An engineering manager forwards a screenshot from a dashboard with low early usage. A leader asks casually in passing, “How is the new launch doing?” Suddenly the ground feels uneven. Every new datapoint, every comment, every stray remark starts to feel like a verdict.

This is normal. Post-launch chaos is not a sign that something is wrong. It is a sign that something is alive. But to navigate this stage well, you have to separate signal from noise. You cannot take every comment at face value. You cannot emotionally absorb every reaction, even though, trust me, you will try to. And this is where experience and maturity play a big role, and you learn this over time on how to compartmentalize and not let it affect you. And you cannot let the loudest voice dictate your roadmap.

Feedback Is Not Insight

Raw feedback is like static on a radio. If you turn the volume up without tuning the frequency, all you hear is noise. People give you surface reactions. They tell you what inconvenienced them today, not the deeper struggle you are actually meant to solve. You have to decode what sits underneath.

To make this real, imagine you just launched a simple automated export tool that replaces a manual spreadsheet workflow. Within 24 hours you get feedback like, “I could not find the download button.” “This did not have all the filters I wanted,” and “This was confusing.” These are reactions. They are not telling you whether the feature reduces effort or eliminates work. They are telling you where the UI created friction. You have to filter those comments correctly.

© Anusha Ravi and Nitika Malhotra 2026
A. Ravi and N. Malhotra, *Launching Enterprise Products*, https://doi.org/10.1007/979-8-8688-2661-0_4

This is also where AI can help you avoid emotional whiplash. Instead of reading every Slack message like it is a verdict, you can route raw feedback into a single place (a doc, Notion, a spreadsheet, or a ticket queue) and use an AI assistant (ChatGPT/Gemini/Notion AI) to summarize: "What are the top themes? What are the top recurring phrases? What is pure confusion vs. a missing workflow?" The goal is not to outsource judgment. The goal is to reduce cognitive load so you can think clearly. It is very easy to get overwhelmed at this stage, but here is where you can use these tricks and filter the noise out. Now, in addition to these, I have a few favorite methodologies that I like to use at this stage to distill clarity directly from customers. I call these my keep-me-from-insanity buttons.

Usability feedback: Picture an analyst opening your new report builder and saying, "I expected the category filter to be on the left," or "I did not know that this button completed the action." This feedback points to interface clarity, not to the usefulness of the underlying functionality. You fix this through design tweaks, content changes, or clearer onboarding.

Here are some examples that you may encounter in your context.

- A payroll admin clicks "Run Preview" thinking it runs payroll, panics, and messages support. Nothing is broken. The label is ambiguous. You rename it to "Preview Only" and add a confirmation step.
- A customer success manager cannot find "Export CSV" because it lives under a kebab menu. They assume it does not exist and escalate. You move export to the primary action area for the first 30 days post-launch and measure whether support tickets drop.
- A procurement analyst says, "This is confusing," but session replay shows they keep hovering on a tooltip and abandoning at the same step. You add inline helper text and a 20-second guided walkthrough.
- A leader forwards a screenshot: "Usage is low." But a quick path analysis shows users are getting stuck on permissions before they even reach the feature. That is not a product value issue. It is a funnel issue.

How to leverage AI here

Use an AI meeting notes tool (Zoom note-taker / Teams recap) to capture verbatims from early enablement calls, then have an LLM categorize them into "label confusion," "navigation," "permissions," and "onboarding gaps" and generate a punch list of micro-fixes. Pair that with behavioral tools (event funnels, session replays) so you fix what people actually do, not what they vaguely say.

Value gap feedback: Imagine a team lead saying, "I still had to do half my workflow manually," or "I could not use this to complete my weekly process." This means you either solved the wrong part of the workflow or unintentionally introduced new friction. It is not a UI problem. It is a "jobs to be done" problem.

Here are some examples:

- You launch an "automated export" that generates a file perfectly, but customers still spend 45 minutes cleaning it because key columns are missing (IDs, status codes, timestamps). They do not want an export. They want a usable dataset that matches their downstream process.
- You build a manager dashboard for "visibility," but managers still open spreadsheets because the dashboard does not support their real ritual: weekly exception review, drill-down to root cause, and a way to assign follow-ups. The dashboard is a picture, not a workflow.
- You ship a self-serve onboarding wizard for a complex integration. Users complete the wizard, but then engineering teams still get pulled in because the final step requires internal API keys and security approvals. You reduced one part of the pain, but the bottleneck lives elsewhere.
- A sales team says "customers are not adopting," but your analysis shows customers are using it, just not in the way you expected. They are using a single subset of the flow repeatedly because that is the only part that removes real work. That is your value wedge.

How to leverage AI here: Take 20–30 pieces of value-gap feedback, feed them into NotebookLM (or an internal doc + AI assistant), and ask, "What job are they hiring this for? What is the 'before' workflow? What step still forces manual work?" Then have ChatGPT generate 3- to 5-candidate JTBD statements and hypotheses you can validate in user calls. AI will not decide the roadmap, but it will help you see patterns faster and articulate the job more crisply.

Expectation mismatch: This happens constantly in enterprise. You might launch a forecasting dashboard meant to provide directional visibility. But someone expected it to be a fully automated predictive engine. They say, "This tool does not forecast accurately." In reality, it was never meant to forecast anything at all. The mismatch comes from positioning, not functionality.

- You ship "role-based access" for a feature, and a security stakeholder assumes it includes full audit trails and SCIM provisioning. They say "This is not enterprise-ready." What they actually want is compliance posture, not access control.
- You launch "automated reminders" (basic rules + notifications), and a VP calls it "AI" in an all-hands. Suddenly customers expect natural language, personalization, and predictive scheduling. The feature is fine. The story inflated the expectation.
- You introduce a "data quality score" that is directional (green/yellow/red), and a customer assumes it is statistically rigorous and defensible for audits. They push back because they think you are making claims you never made. Your issue is messaging, disclaimers, and training—more than engineering.

How to leverage AI here: Use ChatGPT to rewrite your release notes and internal enablement message in three versions: (1) what it is, (2) what it is not, and (3) when to use it. Then use the same tool to generate a short "talk track" for sales and customer success so everyone describes the feature consistently. Expectation mismatch usually begins as a messaging bug. AI can help you patch it fast.

Most feedback fits cleanly into one of these three buckets. Sorting early prevents chaos.

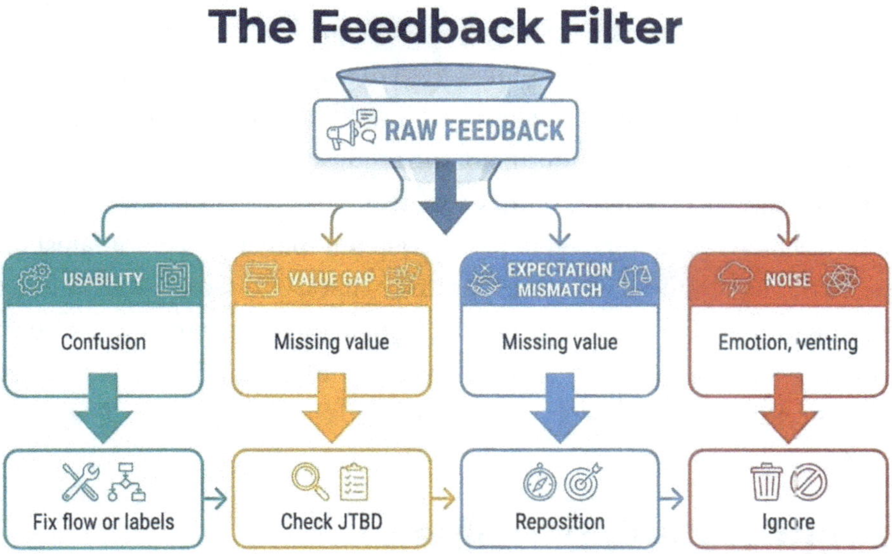

Figure 4-1. *The Feedback Filter*

AI shortcut for the filter (when you are drowning): Paste raw feedback (Slack snippets, call notes, ticket text) into ChatGPT and ask it to tag each line into the four buckets, with a one-sentence rationale and a confidence score. You will still review and override tags—but this gives you a first pass in minutes, not hours. Then you can sort the doc, spot the clusters, and decide what is truly repeated versus what is just loud.

Do Not Let the Loudest Voice Write Your Roadmap

There will always be that moment when someone senior hears a single piece of negative feedback and says, "Should we pause and rethink?" You will feel panic rise in your chest. Again, this is normal. This is where you anchor yourself. Then remind yourself that this is your product; you know the ins and outs of this like no one else. Remind the room of what you launched and why you scoped it that way. Remind them that an MVP is meant to test hypotheses, not to be a fully polished solution. Explain the early signals you are watching. Share what you are learning, not just what you are hearing.

For example, after launching a new customer survey builder, you might hear from one executive that customers are not filling surveys quickly. But your telemetry may show that customers spent less time setting them up, and completion rates improved for the teams who adopted early. The loudest complaint is not the full story. You have to ground leadership in the larger pattern, not the loudest anecdote.

How to leverage AI with leadership pressure: When a leader drops a drive-by "How is it Going?," use an AI assistant to generate a crisp one-pager from your latest metrics and notes: "What we shipped, what we expected, what we're seeing, what we're doing next." Keep the format consistent every week. If you feed it the same inputs (funnel metrics, top feedback themes, decision log), AI can draft the update, and you just edit for accuracy. This reduces reactive storytelling and keeps you anchored to facts.

Make Your Listening Visible

People rarely believe that product teams are listening, even when you are. In fact, the absence of visible follow-up often becomes the source of frustration, more than the product itself. One of the highest-leverage things you can do is create a visible feedback board. This can be as simple as a weekly message to stakeholders summarizing what was heard, what is being explored, and what decisions have been made. It shows that their input matters and that you are not making decisions in a black box.

For example, if multiple customer success managers reported that customers were confused about the placement of a validation step, you capture it on the feedback board, explain that design is evaluating a few options, and share when the decision will land. Suddenly, people feel involved rather than ignored.

How to leverage AI to make listening visible (without spending your life writing updates): Use your meeting transcript tool (Zoom/Teams), your support queue exports, and your Slack highlights as inputs. Drop them into NotebookLM or a single "Launch Listening Doc," then ask an AI assistant to produce three sections: (1) Top 5 themes (tagged by the filter buckets), (2) What we're doing this week, (3) What we're not doing and why. Then copy-paste into your weekly stakeholder post. The board becomes reliable, fast, and consistent—because you are not rebuilding it from scratch every time.

Double Down on the People Who Are Using It

It is incredibly tempting to obsess over drop-off. The moment someone says, "My team stopped using the feature," you want to jump into panic mode. Resist that urge. When usage is low in the beginning, the most important cohort is not the one that dropped off, but the one that stayed.

Imagine you rolled out a new data ingestion workflow. One department immediately embraced it and sent three enthusiastic messages about how it eliminated their manual reconciliation. Another department barely touched it. A third reverted to their old process after one try.

Your instinct might be to fix adoption for the two groups that did not continue. Instead, start with the group that did. Watch exactly how they are using it. They will show you what value clicked, what problem was truly solved, and which parts of the onboarding worked. Those are the insights that scale. Those are the insights that drive your next iteration.

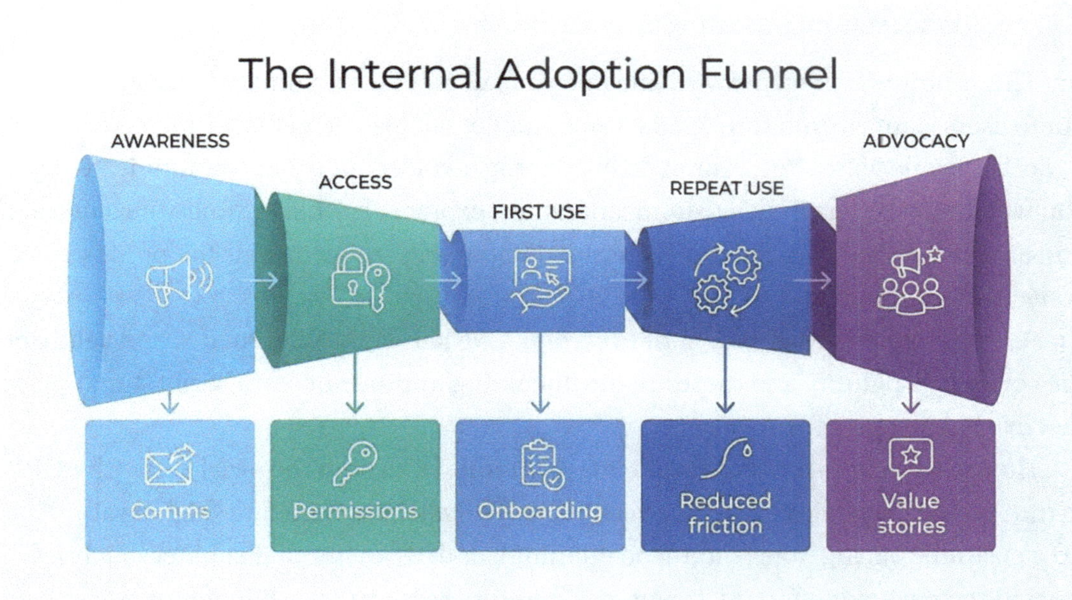

Figure 4-2. *The Internal Adoption Funnel*

Enterprise adoption almost always breaks between first use and repeat use. That is where your next set of improvements should focus.

How to leverage AI with your early adopters (the fastest path to signal): Take transcripts from 5 to 10 "successful user" sessions and ask ChatGPT, "What did they do first? What moment made them say 'oh this helps'? What workaround did they still need?" Then ask it to generate: (a) a simple adoption playbook ("Do these 3 steps first"), (b) a short internal enablement guide for customer success, and (c) 2- to 3-value stories you can reuse in exec updates. Early adopters hand you the narrative—and AI helps you package it.

Decide, Then Communicate

At some point, you will have collected enough feedback to make decisions. You have to be able to articulate three things clearly:

1. What you are fixing immediately.
2. What you are intentionally deferring.
3. What you are not acting on and why.

This is how you prevent swirl. Imagine you launched an automated alerting feature. Some users want custom thresholds, some want email instead of Slack, and some want a way to disable alerts. You cannot do everything at once. But if you communicate that you will prioritize threshold customization now, explore channel flexibility next quarter, and are intentionally not building a disabled option because it defeats the purpose, the conversation stabilizes.

A simple narrative helps anchor everyone. "We launched X, learned Y, and validated the core usage pattern, and these are the upcoming improvements." Clarity stops reactive behavior across the org.

How to leverage AI to communicate decisions (and stop the swirl): Ask ChatGPT to turn your decision log into three versions: (1) a stakeholder update (high level), (2) a customer-facing note (careful positioning), and (3) an internal engineering brief (specific scope, tradeoffs, and acceptance criteria). Same truth—different packaging. This keeps your messaging consistent while matching each audience's needs.

Summary

Feedback is not insight. Treat it as raw input that must be decoded. Do not let the loudest voice dictate your strategy. Make your listening visible and structured. Study your early adopters because they reveal the real shape of the value you created. And once you decide what to do next, communicate that with confidence and intention.

Post-launch chaos should not destabilize you. It is simply the noise that happens when a new idea enters a real environment. Stay calm, observe the patterns, and move with clarity. That is how you move from first launch to lasting impact.

Summary

CHAPTER 5

Navigating Internal Resistance (And Surviving the Politics)

You have launched your first version. You have collected early signals. You are starting to scope the next set of improvements. You are feeling like momentum is finally taking shape. Then suddenly, without warning, resistance hits. Not from customers. Not from users. From inside your own organization. And suddenly you feel like the rug is being pulled under your feet. A leader wants to "revisit scope." Another team says your feature overlaps with something they had planned. Someone starts a parallel initiative with similar goals without looping you in. A cross-functional partner raises concerns about risks you thought were already resolved. It all feels a bit much.

This is not incompetence. This is enterprise gravity. The moment something starts to matter, the organization reacts. Some reactions are helpful. Many feel like blockers. A few can feel political or even territorial. None of this means you made a wrong move. It simply means you have reached the stage where your product creates real change and change triggers friction. Your job now is to understand this resistance, decode its source, and navigate it without losing momentum.

Do Not Take Resistance Personally

The worst mistake you can make is to interpret resistance as a personal judgment. Internal resistance is rarely about you. It is almost always about how change affects someone else's world. Someone's workflow changes. Someone's ownership feels reduced. Someone's team becomes accountable for a new process. Someone who used to be the hero in the old system becomes unnecessary in the new one.

© Anusha Ravi and Nitika Malhotra 2026
A. Ravi and N. Malhotra, *Launching Enterprise Products*, https://doi.org/10.1007/979-8-8688-2661-0_5

Imagine you launch a new automated quality check for data ingestion. A team that previously spent hours manually validating files may worry that their value in the org is reduced. They might frame their resistance as "the tool is not reliable" or "we need to pause until process alignment happens." Underneath the words is a fear that their role is changing.

Or imagine you ship a dashboard that allows business users to get insights directly. Suddenly, the analytics team that used to field these requests may feel bypassed. They might say the dashboard is "too simplistic" or "not validated through central reporting guidelines." Their resistance is not about the dashboard. The resistance is about shifting influence. Once you see the underlying dynamic, the emotional weight disappears. You stop reacting defensively. You start responding strategically.

Diagnose the "Why" Behind the Pushback

Every instance of resistance has a root cause. And the cause is the secret to resolving it.

Here are the five most common causes of enterprise resistance:

1. **Loss of Control:** This is one of the most common ones, and it is almost never said out loud. Control in an enterprise is safety. It is how teams manage accountability and reduce surprise. If a partner team used to be the gatekeeper for a workflow, even a well-meaning self-serve experience can feel like you are removing their ability to prevent bad outcomes. So they start asking for more approvals, more reviews, more governance, and more "alignment," not because they love process, but because they are trying to restore predictability. Real-life example: You introduce a self-serve access request flow that removes a manual approval step, and security pushes back, saying every request must still be reviewed "for now." Underneath, they are imagining an audit and asking themselves who gets blamed. The move is not to argue. The move is to give them new control that does not block progress, like role-based tiers, guardrails, clear audit logs, and escalation paths, so their risk posture stays intact while the workflow still modernizes.

2. **Fear of Mistakes Being Attributed to Them:** This is blame and fear, and it drives a shocking amount of behavior. People resist not because they think your feature is bad, but because they can already see the incident ticket with their name on it. That is why pushback often sounds like "too risky," "we need to wait," "we need more validation," or "we need to socialize more," even when everyone agrees the customer pain is real. Real-life example: Customer success resists rollout because they know their team will be flooded with questions if onboarding is unclear. Another example: An engineering manager says no because their team is on call, and they do not want a 2 a.m. page caused by a new dependency. The fix is to reduce perceived blame with safety design. Bring a phased rollout, monitoring, clear rollback, ownership for support and escalation, and explicit boundaries on what the feature will and will not do in V1. When people see that failure modes have been anticipated, resistance drops fast.

3. **Misalignment on Goals:** This is where everyone uses the same words but means different things. "Speed" means one thing to a product. "Stability" means another thing to the platform. "Customer impact" means something else to sales. In an enterprise, incentives are not aligned by default; they are aligned through rituals and explicit tradeoffs. Real-life example: You are pushing to ship a workflow that touches core infrastructure, but the infra team is measured this quarter on a migration with zero incidents. They are not resisting your product; they are protecting their OKR and their performance review. Another example: A leader tells you "Adoption is the priority," but a partner org is measured on cost reduction, so they resist anything that increases support load. Your move is to translate your initiative into their language, show how it supports their goals, and be clear about what you are not asking them to compromise. If you cannot align goals fully, you align expectations, so your launch does not become a silent conflict that drags for months.

4. **Overlapping Charters:** This is where resistance starts to feel political, because sometimes it is. Two teams believe they own the same territory, or they believe they should. In large organizations, this happens constantly because org structures shift, roadmaps evolve, and platform teams naturally want to centralize. Overlap creates fear of lost credit, lost budget, lost influence, and future ownership ambiguity. Real-life example: You build a lightweight case management experience for your product, and a central platform team says "We are building case management." Even if your scope is narrow and theirs is broader, they worry customers will associate the capability with you and bypass their platform. Another example: You ship a dashboard for business users, and the analytics team says it conflicts with reporting standards. Sometimes that is a real governance point. Sometimes it is about influence. The move is to clarify boundaries early. Name the domain, name the ownership, name what you are building now, name what you will not build, and offer an integration path so both teams win. When you leave overlap vague, you invite turf wars. When you make boundaries explicit, you create room for collaboration.

5. **Bandwidth Anxiety:** This is the polite version of resistance, and it is often the most honest. People are overloaded, and your initiative is one more thing. The reason it still becomes political is that nobody wants to say, "I do not have capacity," so they wrap it in reasons that sound more legitimate, like "we need more requirements," "we need to rethink the approach," "this is not the right time," or "this is not prioritized." Real-life example: A QA team resists because the release window is already packed and they cannot take on additional testing, but they frame it as "the scope is unclear." Or a design partner pushes back because they are already committed to another flagship initiative and cannot do a full redesign, so they call your UX "not ready." Your move is to treat bandwidth as a constraint, not as a character flaw. You

reduce scope, offer phased delivery, bring templates, bring clearer requirements, and sometimes you bring help, like writing the first draft of test plans, providing analytics instrumentation specs, or doing the coordination work so the ask becomes smaller. When people feel the request is survivable, they stop resisting.

For instance, if engineering says, "We cannot build this right now," the root cause may not be technical at all. It might be fear that if they take this on, they will miss a critical OKR tied to their performance reviews and tech org goals. If legal pushes back, the root cause might be unclear risk boundaries. If customer success hesitates, it might be fear of being overwhelmed with questions during rollout.

Understanding the true "why" helps you adjust your approach instead of escalating tension.

Not All Resistance Is Bad

A surprising truth: some resistance is extremely valuable. It tells you where your assumptions did not hold. It surfaces risks you did not consider. It highlights dependencies that were not visible. Sometimes, resistance saves you from a bad decision.

Imagine you are planning to fully automate a workflow. A skeptical partner from operations might ask, "Who handles exceptions?" Their resistance feels like pushback, but in reality, they unveiled a gap in your process design. Or an architecture lead pushes back on your integration plan. They might appear obstructive, but they are pointing to a scalability issue that would have broken the system six months later.

Resistance, when understood correctly, is an early warning system.

How AI tools can help you navigate resistance without burning your time and energy: When resistance shows up, your biggest challenge is not intelligence. It is fragmentation. The feedback is scattered across Slack, meetings, docs, tickets, and side conversations. AI helps you consolidate, structure, and move the conversation from emotion to clarity. The real win is that you stop debating vibes and start aligning on a shared map. Tools like FigJam, Miro, and Mural are especially powerful here because they turn messy input into something visual, shareable, and hard to argue with. Here are practical ways to use them in this chapter in real life. Use AI to diagnose the resistance in real time. After a tough meeting, paste the raw notes into ChatGPT or Gemini and ask it to tag each concern into the five causes: loss of control, fear of blame, misalignment on goals, overlapping charters, and bandwidth anxiety. Then ask it to propose the next best move for each one, like "add guardrails," "clarify ownership," "bring to governance," "phase rollout," or "do a co-design session." You still apply judgment, but AI gives you a fast first pass and saves you from spiraling. Use FigJam, Miro, or Mural AI templates to make the invisible visible. Resistance is easier to resolve when people can see the system.

Use AI-driven sticky note clustering to take dozens of comments and group them into themes. Then label the clusters with the root causes. This is not for theatrics. This creates a neutral artifact that stops people from repeating the same arguments in circles. Use an AI-powered stakeholder map to reveal the real influence network. In FigJam or Miro, start with a simple stakeholder map template. Then use AI to help you generate the list of stakeholders, their incentives, what they fear, what they control, and what they need to say yes. Once you see that the loudest resistor is not always the most powerful one, your strategy gets sharper. This is how you stop fighting the wrong battles. Use AI to draft alignment artifacts fast. Most enterprise resistance gets solved through writing, not debating. Use ChatGPT to generate a one-page decision narrative that includes the problem, the constraints, what is changing, what is not changing, guardrails, and the rollout plan. Then paste that into your governance forums and stakeholder threads.

When people see clear boundaries, resistance drops. Use AI-assisted workshop facilitation to turn critics into co-creators. If you have a critic who keeps blocking, do not keep arguing in meetings. Run a structured workshop. Use a FigJam or Miro template for "Risks and mitigations" or "Ways of working" or "RACI and ownership." Then use AI to generate prompts for the workshop, a suggested agenda, and even follow-up action items. Critics calm down when they are given a legitimate structure to contribute. Use AI summarizers to protect your time. After every messy alignment thread, use an AI assistant to produce a clean summary with three sections: what we agree on, what is unresolved, and next steps with owners. Then you post that as the official recap. This is how you prevent endless debates. It is also how you reduce politics, because written summaries create accountability without confrontation.

Use Empathy As a Tactical Tool

Empathy is not softness. It is strategy. When someone resists change, your first response should be curiosity. What pain are they anticipating? What risk are they carrying? What incentives are they accountable to? When you reflect their concern back to them, you lower the temperature instantly.

Imagine a product meeting where the platform team says, "We cannot support this release due to upcoming infra migrations." Instead of pushing back, you respond with, "It sounds like the risk window is tight, and we could disrupt your migration if we launch during that period. Help me understand your constraints so we can adjust."

This completely changes the tone of the conversation. You are not fighting them. You are partnering with them.

Empathy prevents escalation. Empathy creates allies.

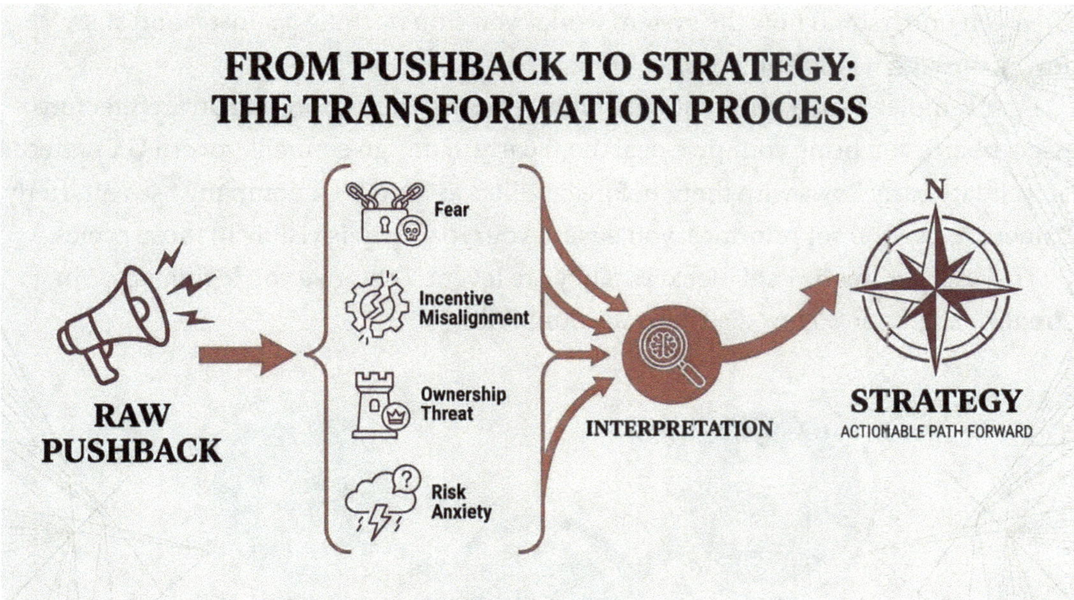

Figure 5-1. *From Pushback to Strategy*

Activate Critics into Co-Creators

There is a counterintuitive truth about internal critics. The ones who complain the most often become your strongest champions if you include them early and meaningfully. People who care enough to resist usually have strong context and strong opinions. If you bring them into the solution, they shift from obstacle to advocate.

Imagine you are building a new workflow automation and a data science partner keeps raising concerns about edge cases. Instead of avoiding them, you offer, "Can we walk through the edge cases together and co-design the fallback logic." Once they feel ownership in the solution, they support the project instead of blocking it.

The moment a critic contributes to the solution, they become invested in its success. This is one of the easiest ways to convert resistance into alignment.

Use the System to Navigate the System

In large enterprises, decisions are not made only through conversations. They are made through rituals, governance bodies, documentation trails, and cross-functional forums. When you understand how the system works, you stop pushing against it and start moving through it efficiently.

For example, if you know that major initiatives must pass through an architecture review board, you bring your proposal there early. If design councils govern UX patterns, you validate early flows with them before conflicts arise. If your company uses quarterly business reviews to set priorities, you ensure your roadmap is visible in those cycles.

These structures are not blockers. They are levers. They give you legitimacy. They formalize alignment. They distribute accountability.

Figure 5-2. *Stakeholder Map*

Anchor Everything Back to the Problem

When you feel like you are being pulled into politics, conflict, or tension, it is easy to lose your grounding. Bring the conversation back to the source. What problem are we solving? What pain are customers feeling? What business outcome matters here? What happens if we do nothing? That objectivity resets the room.

If someone says, "We should stop the release," you respond with, "Let us revisit the customer problem we are solving and the impact of delaying. If we delay by three months, here is the cost. If we move forward with guardrails, here is the gain. Which tradeoff do we prefer."

This removes emotion and restores clarity.

Summary

Internal resistance is not a red flag. It is a natural part of driving change in an enterprise. Do not take it personally. Diagnose the root cause. Use empathy to reduce tension. Turn critics into collaborators. Navigate the organization's decision structures intentionally. And always reground the conversation in the customer problem and business value.

Momentum must be earned, but traction must be protected. When you master the art of navigating internal resistance, you do not just ship features. You shift how the organization moves.

CHAPTER 6

Driving Adoption Without Forcing It

You have launched the MVP. You have collected feedback. You have navigated the internal politics that inevitably surface when something new enters the system. Now you arrive at the part that sounds simple in theory but is easily one of the hardest parts of enterprise product building: getting people to actually use the thing.

Many PMs assume that if the feature is good, adoption will follow. It almost never works that way. Adoption is not an outcome. It is a process. You may even say in some ways it's like writing this book. We can do a killer job of writing the book, but if advocacy, intentional marketing, and value driving are not done well, it can go bust. Inside enterprises, adoption is shaped by habits, incentives, competing tools, legacy processes, team behavior, and sometimes even fear. You cannot force adoption. You have to design for it.

Understand the Activation Moment

Every successful product has a moment where something "clicks." The user goes from "What is this" to "Oh, this is useful." This is the activation moment. Without it, adoption is dead on arrival.

In consumer apps, the activation moment is clear. Your first ride is booked. Your first video is uploaded. Your first purchase. Enterprise activation is more subtle. It usually shows up when someone saves meaningful time or avoids a manual process or completes a workflow without needing support or realizes they can now do something faster than before.

For example, imagine you launch a self-service data export tool. The activation moment might not be the first click. It might be the moment a business analyst realizes they pulled a report in 15 seconds that used to require a full-day turnaround from a

© Anusha Ravi and Nitika Malhotra 2026
A. Ravi and N. Malhotra, *Launching Enterprise Products*, https://doi.org/10.1007/979-8-8688-2661-0_6

centralized team. That is when the feature becomes real. Or imagine you introduce a workflow automation that sends alerts when performance drops. The activation moment is not the first alert. It is when a manager says, "This caught an issue before I had to escalate it manually."

Find that moment. Design around that moment. Measure that moment.

How to leverage AI for the activation moment: The activation moment is a pattern problem. You are trying to find the exact moment where value becomes undeniable, and that signal is usually buried in messy data. This is where AI helps you move faster without guessing. Start by collecting three inputs: support tickets, call notes, and usage logs. Then use an AI assistant to extract the phrases that indicate "click," like "this saved me," "I did not need to ask," "this is faster," and "I can finally" and pair those with the exact user actions that happened right before. You are basically reverse engineering value. Real-life example: You see repeated messages like "I did not have to wait on analytics," and AI helps you map it to the sequence: open export, apply filter, preview, download, and share. That becomes your activation path, and you design onboarding around that exact path. Tools that help here in real life are ChatGPT or Gemini for pattern extraction, NotebookLM for building a living knowledge base of what users say, and even basic spreadsheets plus AI formulas if your org supports it. The key is not the tool; it is using AI to connect language to behavior.

Build Enablement into the Product, Not Around It

Product teams love a good enablement deck. Slideware. Tutorials. Video walkthroughs. The problem is that most users never open them. If your product requires extensive training to understand the basics, you already have an adoption problem.

The product must teach itself. It must guide users through the first steps. It must remove friction at the start. It must create confidence without requiring handholding.

Think about a scenario where you launch a new task management module. You could create a detailed onboarding manual, or you could embed tooltips, highlight the first action, show an example task, and guide the user to complete one small workflow successfully. That small success creates momentum more reliably than any training document.

Or imagine introducing a forecasting tool. Users resist forecasting because they believe it is complex. But if your first screen simply asks for three inputs and shows an instant preview, adoption rises because hesitation drops. Enablement is not an event. It is a built-in experience.

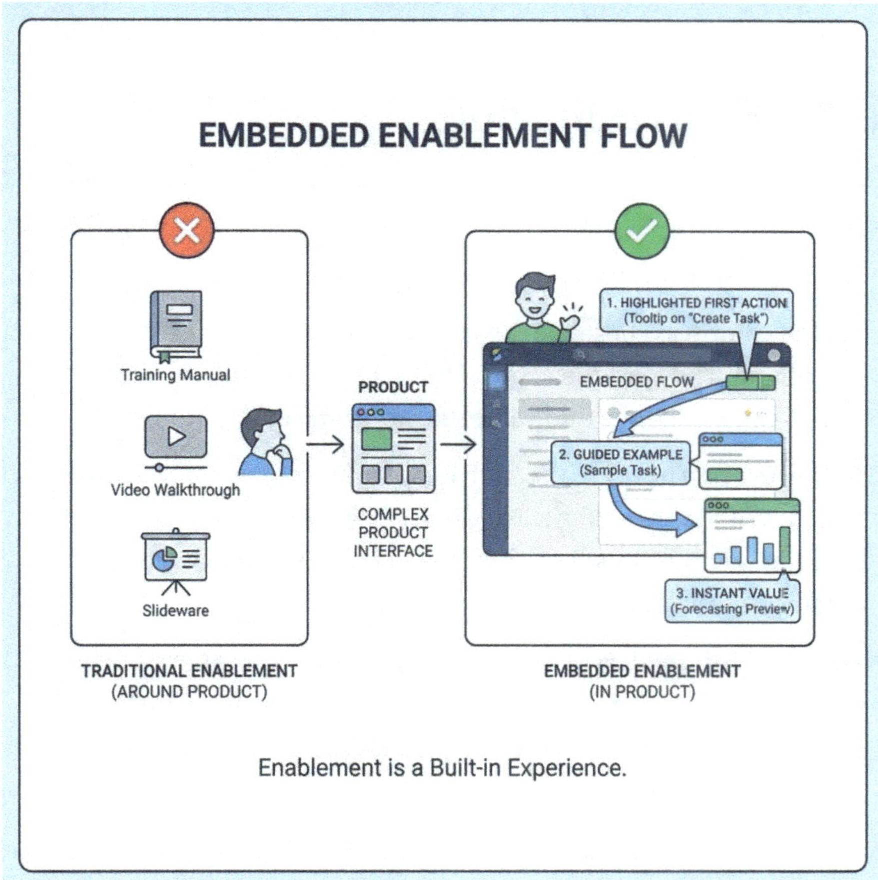

Figure 6-1. *Embedded Enablement Model*

How to leverage AI for embedded enablement: AI can help you write and test enablement faster, especially the microcopy and the guided steps that decide whether someone feels confident or confused. Use ChatGPT to generate multiple versions of tooltips, helper text, empty states, and onboarding nudges in your tone. Then run those variants past a few users or internal partners and keep what lands. You can also use AI to translate the same onboarding into role-based language. What a finance user needs to hear is not what an ops user needs to hear, even if the feature is the same. AI makes it easy to personalize the first-run experience without reinventing everything manually.

This is also where FigJam, Miro, and Mural come in. Use AI-driven templates like journey mapping and onboarding flow builders to visualize the first-time experience. Drop in your steps; ask the AI organizer to cluster friction points, and you will quickly see where users hesitate. The value is not the pretty board. The value is that the whole team can see the onboarding path and agree on what to fix first.

Nudge the Right Behaviors

Adoption does not grow by chasing everyone. It grows by nudging the right users at the right moments.

There are three groups you should focus on:

> **Early explorers**: These are the curious ones. They click everything. They test the edges. They will break things just to see what happens. If they find value, they become early champions.
>
> **Power users**: These are the individuals who convert your feature into part of their workflow. They hack extensions. They ask meaningful questions. They give real feedback. They become organic internal advocates.
>
> **Skeptical influencers**: These are the people with influence inside the org. If they are unsure, the teams around them hesitate. If they feel confident, adoption spreads quickly. You cannot ignore this group. You must bring them along.

For example, imagine launching a new internal insights dashboard. The early explorers will be the ones clicking all the tabs and discovering hidden gems. The power users will start using the dashboard for weekly reporting. The skeptical influencers will not open it unless you personally walk them through how it answers a business-critical question.

Your job is to support all three, but in different ways. Explorers need access. Power users need deeper functionality. Skeptical influencers need to understand purpose and value.

Nudging is not manipulation. It is strategic activation.

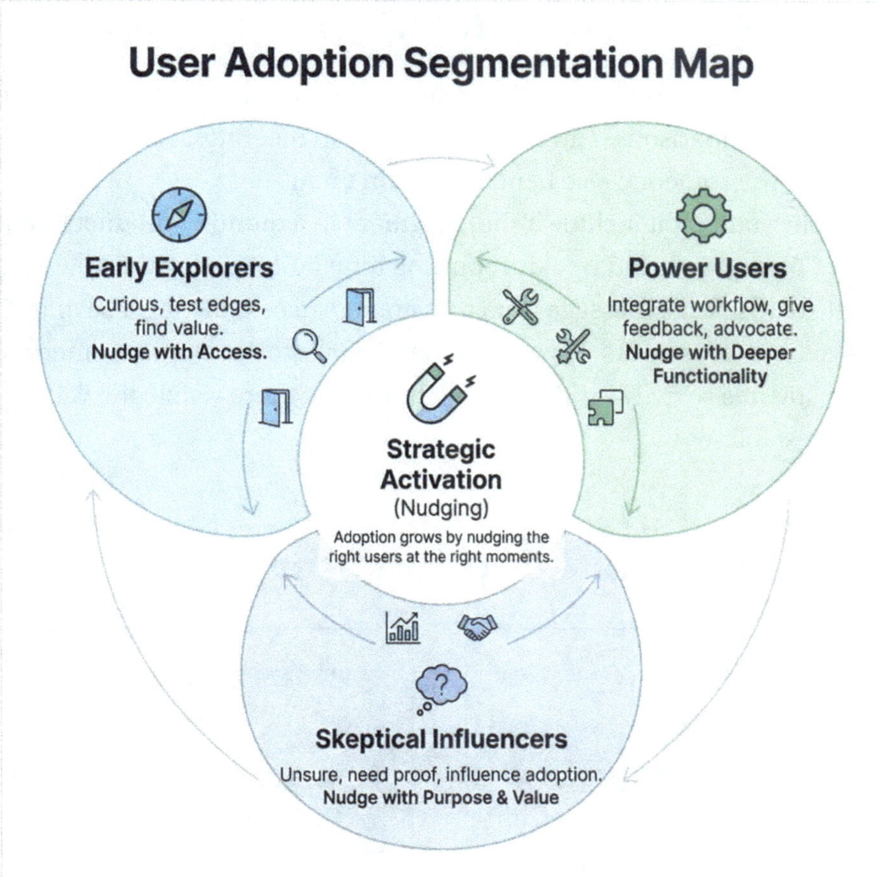

***Figure 6-2.** Internal Adoption Segments*

How to leverage AI to nudge the right behaviors: AI helps you avoid the classic mistake of treating all users the same. Use AI to segment adoption narratives and nudges based on persona and motivation. For early explorers, AI can generate "try this" challenges and quick experiments that encourage discovery. For power users, AI can help create deeper playbooks, shortcuts, and advanced workflows that turn the product into muscle memory. For skeptical influencers, AI can help you craft a tight business narrative that connects the feature to outcomes they already care about. In FigJam, Miro, or Mural, you can use AI templates for persona mapping and influence mapping to identify who actually drives behavior in the org. Then you tailor your rollout plan. This is where adoption becomes less about broadcasting and more about precision. You can also use AI to generate the actual nudge assets at scale, like short Slack messages, quick demo scripts, and one-slide summaries, all aligned to each cohort. The point is not to spam people. The point is to make the first touch feel relevant instead of generic.

Tell the Adoption Story Inside the Company

Adoption does not spread on its own. It spreads through stories, examples, screenshots, before-and-after comparisons, and tiny wins shared in meetings. Teams adopt features faster when they see someone else benefiting from them.

For example, you might include a short segment in a monthly product update showing that "Team A reduced weekly reporting time by 40% using the new module." Or you might share a Slack message from a customer success manager saying, "This workflow saved me three hours this week." These small stories create momentum.

Adoption spreads socially inside organizations. The more visible the value becomes, the faster the rest follow.

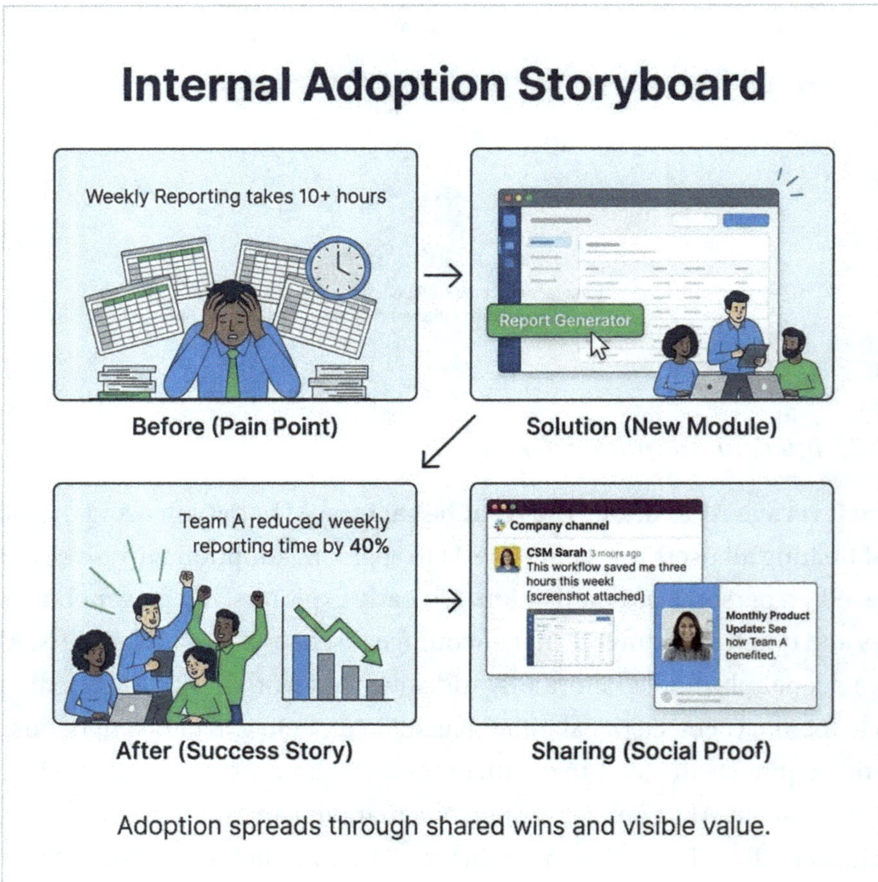

Figure 6-3. *Internal Adoption Storyboard*

How to leverage AI to tell the adoption story: AI is extremely good at turning messy wins into clean narratives. Take screenshots, quotes, and a few metrics, and then ask an AI assistant to draft a story in three formats: a Slack post, a 1-minute talk track for a meeting, and a two-slide update for leaders. Keep the message consistent and repeatable. "We launched X, it removed Y pain, and here is the proof." This matters because adoption is social, and social proof spreads when it is easy to share. This is also where FigJam, Miro, and Mural shine. You can create an "adoption storyboard" board and use AI to organize wins by team, workflow, and impact. Then when someone asks "who is using it," you do not scramble. You pull up the board and show the story. Visibility creates momentum, and momentum creates pull.

Create Pull, Not Pressure

One of the biggest mistakes PMs make is trying to force adoption. They escalate through leadership. They send aggressive nudges. They treat usage as compliance. When you force adoption, teams do the bare minimum. They use the feature only when someone is watching. They resent the tool rather than embrace it.

The alternative is to create pull. Make the product easy to try. Make it safe. Make it obvious how it improves a team's day. Make the first step small and simple.

Imagine launching a new workflow builder. Instead of telling teams, "You must switch," you create a lightweight starter workflow that solves one repetitive pain point. Once they see the benefit, they want more. Or imagine introducing a new insights module. Instead of mandating usage, you show how one team used it to uncover a trend that helped them plan better.

Pull is powerful because it respects autonomy. It builds organic demand.

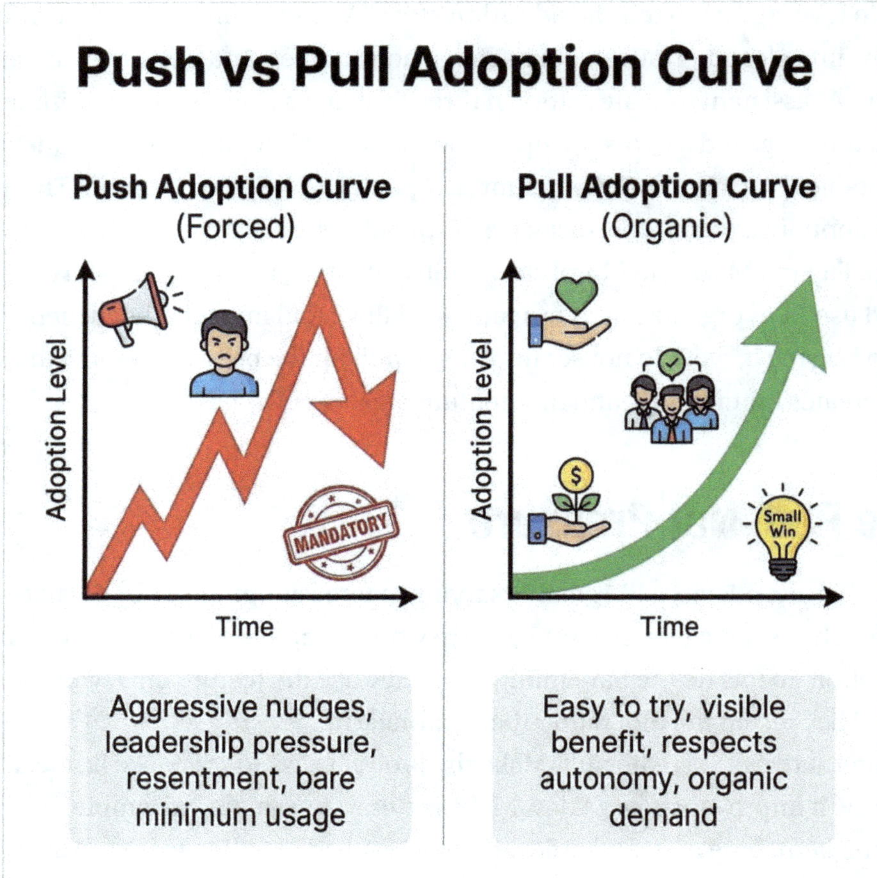

Figure 6-4. *Push vs. Pull Adoption Curve*

How to leverage AI to create pull instead of pressure: Pull is built on confidence and safety. AI can help you design both. First, use AI to identify the smallest "starter win" that delivers value in under ten minutes. Ask it, based on the workflow and constraints, what the simplest entry point is that still feels meaningful. Then design a starter template around that. Second, use AI to anticipate objections and write answers in plain language. People hesitate because they fear messing up, breaking something, or looking incompetent. If you proactively address that fear with clear guardrails, the trial barrier drops. This is where AI-driven templates in tools like Miro, Mural, and FigJam become a force multiplier. Create ready-to-use starter flows, examples, and checklists that teams can clone. A blank state creates paralysis. A template creates motion. And when teams can start from something prebuilt, adoption stops feeling like a big switch and starts feeling like a small experiment. You can also use AI to generate a "safe trial" plan that leaders will support without turning it into compliance. Something like, "Try this for one weekly cycle, compare time spent, share one learning." That is pull, because it is framed as learning and value, not enforcement.

Summary

Driving adoption is not about pushing people into a new workflow. It is about helping them discover its value naturally. Find the activation moment that makes the product "click." Build onboarding inside the product itself. Identify explorers, power users, and skeptical influencers and support each group strategically. Tell the adoption story in a way that spreads naturally across the organization. Create pull, not pressure.

When adoption grows through value instead of force, you do more than launch a product. You change behavior. You shift the culture. And you build something people choose to use even when nobody is watching.

CHAPTER 7

Telling the Right Data Story (When the Numbers Don't Cooperate)

You ship. You refresh the dashboard.

And your heart sinks.

The line is flat. Engagement looks soft. Someone senior asks, "Are we sure this is working?"

Welcome to the most predictable part of 0 to 1. The post-launch data panic.

Enterprise data almost never behaves the way you want in the first few weeks of a new product. Telemetry is half wired. Legacy systems were never designed to see the new behavior. Usage is patchy. The people who actually use the product are busy doing their job, not creating clean time series for your leadership review.

The difference between an anxious PM and a credible PM in this moment is not the numbers. It is the story they tell around them.

In this chapter, we are going to talk about how to tell that story in a way that is honest, grounded, and persuasive, even when the graphs are not singing yet. We will look at how to anchor in the "why," how to define success signals before launch, how to mix numbers with narrative, how to be transparent about gaps without losing trust, and how to package all of this so your story can travel through the organization without you in the room.

© Anusha Ravi and Nitika Malhotra 2026
A. Ravi and N. Malhotra, *Launching Enterprise Products*, https://doi.org/10.1007/979-8-8688-2661-0_7

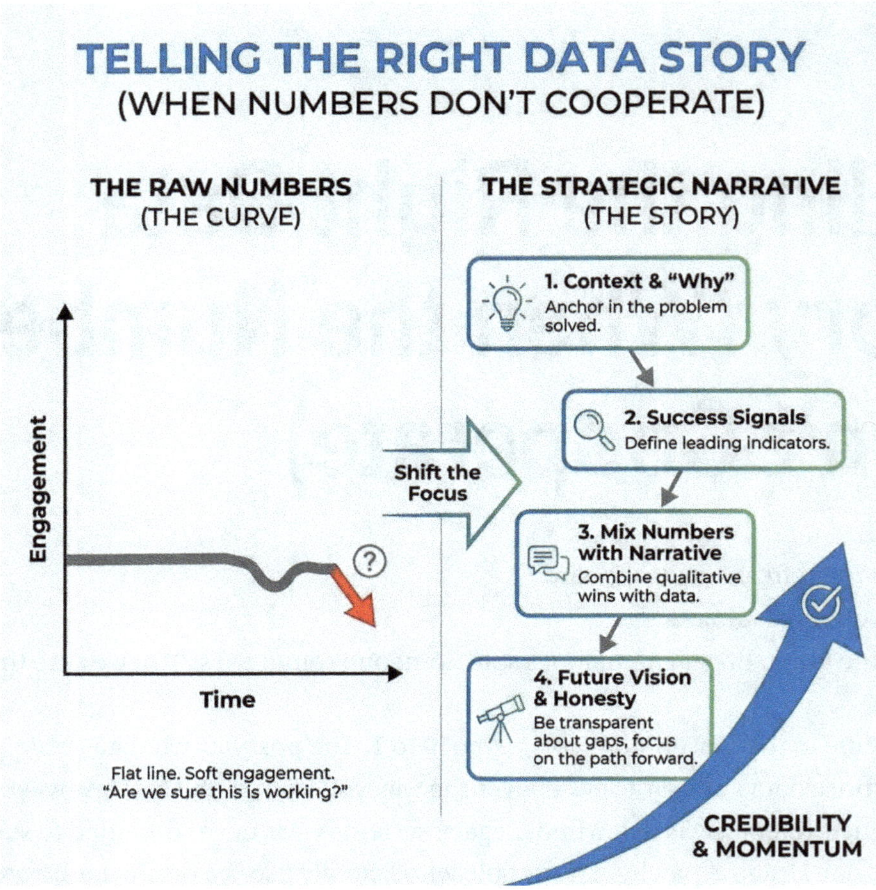

Figure 7-1. *Telling the Right Data Story*

Step 1: Anchor to the Why, Not the Chart

Early data is messy. Your story does not have to be.

When you launch a 0 to 1 product inside an enterprise, the first numbers almost never tell the full truth. This is especially painful when what you have built is infrastructure disguised as a feature.

Take one of our early self-serve tool launches. Until then, sellers had to email complex data files to an internal team, wait days or sometimes weeks for processing, and had zero visibility into whether their data was accepted, rejected, or even opened. The experience was opaque and fragile for everyone involved.

We built the first version of a self-serve activation experience inside the portal. Sellers could now upload, validate, and track their own data in something close to real time. We automated ingestion. We created transparency. We also quietly laid the groundwork for a multiyear roadmap with a multibillion-dollar upside.

Then we looked at the dashboards. Adoption looked flat. Very flat.

If you judged that launch by the basic adoption curve in month one, you would have called it a failure. But this launch was not about mass daily engagement. It was about building the pipes. It changed the foundation for how data could move through the system and who could see its health.

So instead of obsessing over the line chart, we looked at what really moved. Email-based file transfers dropped to zero. Sellers got end-to-end visibility for the first time and stopped asking, "Did my file go through?" Internal teams stopped acting as human routers and started focusing on higher-value work. That invisible shift made it possible to even think about a 5-year plan with a huge revenue opportunity. Without this first launch, that LRP deck would have just been fiction.

This is the uncomfortable truth about a lot of foundational work. The early charts may look boring, but the system underneath just changed permanently.

The same pattern shows up in enterprise SaaS all the time. A security review workflow moves from fragmented email threads into a central platform. The number of "active sessions" barely moves, but review time drops by half and audit findings quietly disappear. If you only stare at the front door metric, you miss the whole point.

When your early graphs are not flattering, you have to go back to the reason the product exists. What business problem did you set out to change? How did work happen before? What did you remove or unlock? Those are your anchors.

The pro tip here is simple. When your first build changes how the work happens, not just who clicks the button, do not let an early adoption curve write the whole story. Start with the "why," then bring the chart in as supporting evidence, not the main character.

This is where AI helps you keep your narrative honest and grounded when leadership is staring at a flat line. The trick is to stop asking the dashboard to answer a question it was never designed to answer. Tools like Amplitude, Mixpanel, Google Analytics, Adobe Analytics, and Pendo are great at capturing behaviors, but early on they are often incomplete, mislabeled, or missing key events. AI helps you bridge that gap by turning scattered signals into a coherent "why" story. A practical move is to use AI to generate a "why first" narrative directly from your inputs.

Pull a few key artifacts, a release note, a launch goal, a couple of customer quotes, and a screenshot of the dashboard, and ask an AI assistant to draft the story anchored in the business problem, what changed in the workflow, and what non-obvious impact you should track. It forces you to separate foundational value from vanity metrics. You can also use AI inside the analytics workflow itself. For example, if your events in Amplitude or Mixpanel are messy, paste the event list into ChatGPT and ask it to propose a clean taxonomy that matches the workflow, like activation events, success events, failure events, and support events. That becomes the foundation for instrumentation fixes, and it also helps you explain to leadership why early metrics may undercount reality.

Step 2: Define Success Signals Before You Ship

Messy data hurts most when you are arguing about what "good" means after the fact. In 0 to 1, you will not have perfect instrumentation. You can at least have intentional framing.

Before you ship, define what success would look like at three levels.

The first is a leading signal. This is the behavior change you would expect to see quickly if your bet is right. For example, more users completing a setup flow without help, sellers submitting structured files instead of email attachments, or managers generating a specific report without pinging an analyst. These are often countable actions or funnel completions that move faster than pure revenue.

The second is a lagging signal. This is the measurable impact that you expect over a slightly longer horizon. That might be reduced cycle time, fewer errors, lower support volume, or increased attach rate. These are the metrics that show up in quarterly reviews and annual plans. They tend to move slower, but they are harder to argue with once they do.

The third is sentiment. This is the qualitative proof that the product is changing how people feel about the work. A customer saying, "This finally saves us hours," or an internal user saying, "I cannot imagine going back to the old way." You collect these through interviews, surveys, Slack messages, ticket comments, and informal conversations.

You do not need to turn this into a 40-page analytics plan. You do need to write down, "For this launch, our leading signal is X, our lagging signal is Y, and we will collect these three types of user feedback for sentiment." That is enough to orient everyone.

If you wait until after launch to decide what success is, you will spend your next review arguing over which metric counts. One stakeholder will point to logins. Another will point to NPS. A third will dig up a random spike in something else and call it evidence. Clarity on success signals upfront lets you avoid that chaos later.

You see this done well in some internal data platform launches. Before they ever roll out a new self-serve query tool, the team aligns on a leading signal like "number of non-technical users successfully running saved queries" and a lagging signal like "reduction in ad hoc data requests to the analytics team." When the charts come in, everyone already knows which curves to pay attention to. There is less drama and more learning.

AI is great at forcing clarity before you ship. Give ChatGPT or Gemini the product goal, the workflow, the user roles, and the constraints and ask it to propose three leading signals, three lagging signals, and three sentiment prompts. Then pick one or two that truly match the bet you are making. The outcome is not a longer document. The outcome is a sharper definition of success. In tools like Amplitude and Mixpanel, you can map these signals directly into funnels and cohorts. AI can help you draft the event plan and instrumentation checklist in plain language, like "user starts upload," "user passes validation," "user resolves error," and "user completes submission," "user tracks status." Even if engineering instruments only have 70% of it at launch, you have a clear target, and you can explain what is missing without sounding fuzzy. For Pendo specifically, AI becomes powerful when you pair your success signals to in-product guides. If the leading signal is "completed setup without help," your Pendo guide should literally shepherd people to that moment. Your analytics and your enablement become one integrated strategy, not separate workstreams.

Step 3: Mix Quant with Qual

Numbers tell you what happened. Stories tell you why it matters. You need both.

Every chart you show should come with some qualitative context. This is not decoration. It is how you translate raw behavior into real-world meaning.

You can think about it in three small buckets. First, direct quotes. These are things users actually said about the product or workflow. For example, "This feature cut my manual work by half" or "I finally understand what happened to my file." Second, before and after stories. You describe how a task used to work and how it works now. For example, "It used to take ten steps and three different tools to complete this request. Now it takes three steps in one place." Third, observational insights. You look at patterns in usage and connect them to actual behavior. For example, "Teams used the export function four times more than we expected, which tells us they are sharing these reports widely outside the system."

You attach these to the numbers. If you show a chart of weekly active users, you add, "Most of this early traffic is coming from five power users in region A who are running workflows daily while other regions are still onboarding." If you show a graph of completed jobs, you add, "Many of these jobs used to be processed manually. Here is how much time that changes for one team."

At one internal rollout of a workflow engine, the early daily active user numbers looked low. On the surface, it looked like a soft launch. Then the team actually talked to the users and realized they had built automations that ran without human babysitting. People logged in less often because the system was doing the work for them. DAU went down. Business impact went up. That is narrative gold, and you only find it by combining numbers with context.

The point is not to spin the data. The point is to give it depth. When you pair quantitative and qualitative signals, you stop arguing about whether a single metric is "good" and start understanding what it really says about behavior.

This is where AI saves you hours and makes your story stronger. Pull qualitative inputs, Slack messages, support tickets, and call transcripts and put them into an AI assistant and ask it to extract themes and representative quotes. Then connect those themes back to the numbers in your analytics tool. You are basically building a bridge from behavior to meaning. Amplitude and Mixpanel help you find the "what" with funnels, retention, and cohorts. AI helps you explain the "why" by turning messy text into clean insight. For example, you see a funnel drop between validation and submission. AI summarizes the top ten user complaints, and you realize most of them are confusion about one required field. That is a usability fix, not a value failure. Your chart becomes actionable instead of scary. Pendo is also useful here because it gives you in-app behavior plus feedback prompts. AI can help you draft micro-surveys that are actually diagnostic, like "What stopped you today?" with smart options that map to your funnel steps. Then you can quantify the qual, which makes leadership conversations much calmer.

Step 4: Be Transparent About Gaps

Executives can smell spin very quickly. Once they think you are massaging the truth, your charts become background noise.

A cleaner strategy is to be brutally transparent about the limitations of your data while still being confident in your interpretation.

If you have partial telemetry, say that clearly. "We are seeing 25 percent of eligible teams using the feature weekly. There are gaps in how legacy modules log activity, which likely undercounts some usage. We have an instrumentation fix in progress this quarter." That is honest, specific, and responsible.

Do not say, "Adoption is strong, but some data is missing" and then click away from the slide. That reads as defensive, even if you do not mean it that way.

You can use phrases like, "This is an early read, not the final word," and "Here is what we can say with confidence today, and here is what we will be able to say once the remaining pieces are wired." Those small sentences buy you trust and time.

Transparency also extends to what is not working. If a bet is not landing the way you expected, say so. Explain what you are learning from it and what you plan to change. Calm, grounded honesty looks far more credible than forced enthusiasm over a weak signal.

In one enterprise SaaS company, an internal AI assistant was rolled out with a lot of hype. The early usage numbers were noisy. Some logs were missing. Some teams were not using it at all. The PM did not pretend it was a runaway success. Instead, they showed a clear view of where it was being used, admitted where telemetry was thin, and paired that with specific stories from the teams who had integrated it into their daily work. That mix of clarity and humility made leadership more willing to fund the next iteration, not less.

You are not expected to have perfect data. You are expected to have a clear view of what the data can and cannot say.

This is where AI can help you be transparent without sounding weak. Use it to draft a clean "data limitations" paragraph that is specific, non-defensive, and action-oriented. For example, "Here is what is fully instrumented, here is what is partially instrumented, here is what is not captured, and here is the fix with timing." That is credibility. You can also use AI to sanity check whether your interpretation is reasonable. Share the key metrics, the known gaps, and the user context and ask the model, "What are three plausible explanations for this pattern that are not 'the product failed.'" It helps you avoid premature conclusions and gives you a better set of follow-up questions for your analytics team. In tools like Adobe Analytics and Google Analytics, event definitions and filters can silently cause undercounting. AI can help you spot obvious issues faster by reviewing the tagging plan and pointing out missing events, duplicated events, or misaligned naming. You still validate with your analytics partner, but you show up sharper.

Step 5: Make the Story Easy to Share

Data does not move through dashboards. It moves through conversations.

If your VP cannot retell your story in their own words when they walk into another meeting, you have lost control of the narrative. You want your updates to be concise enough and concrete enough that they can survive multiple retellings without turning into a game of telephone.

A simple format that works very well is a three-line story. First line: what you launched. Second line: what you are seeing. Third line: what it means and what happens next. For example:

"We launched the self-serve reporting feature for partner teams. Thirty eight percent of active accounts now automate their weekly reports instead of running them manually. This has cut 250 analyst hours per quarter, and next we are adding custom exports and training two more regions."

That is the kind of story a senior leader can repeat in a planning discussion without needing your slide deck. It contains the product, the signal, and the implication in one small package.

You can think of your review as building a "data storyboard" instead of just a report. Each slide or section answers one simple piece of the larger narrative. Here is what we launched. Here is who is using it. Here is what is changing because of it. Here is what we still do not know. Here is what we will do next.

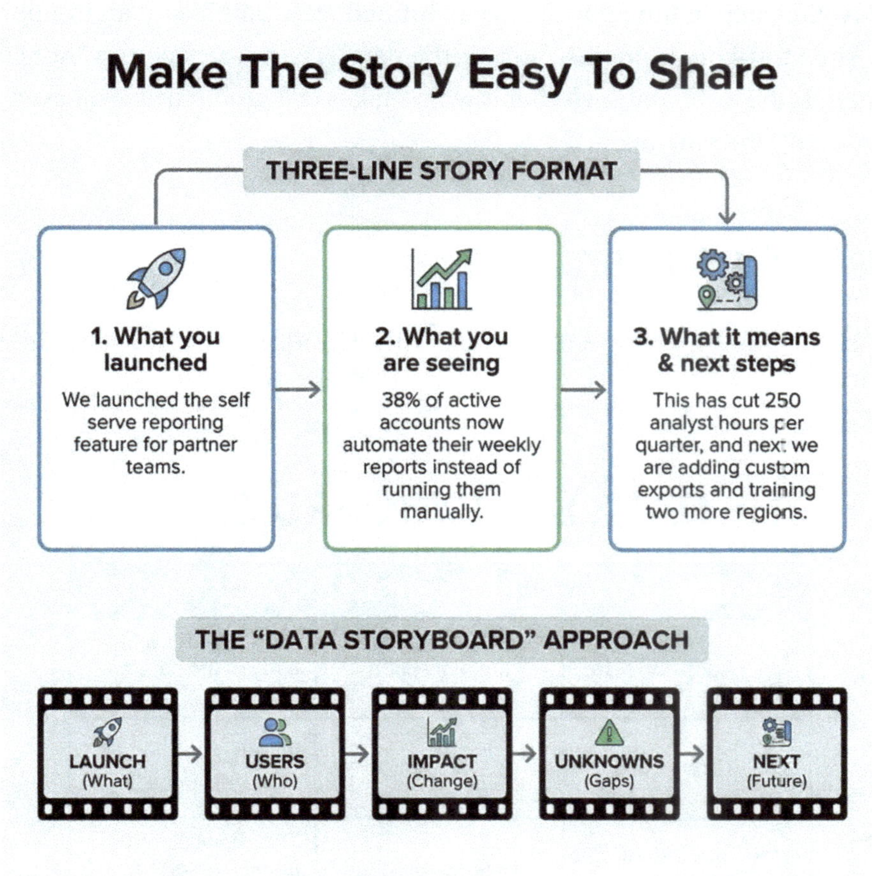

Figure 7-2. *Three-Line Story Format*

AI is your packaging engine. Once you have the inputs, it can generate consistent outputs fast. You feed it your three-line story, your key metric, one quote, one gap, and one next step and ask it to produce versions for different audiences. A leader version, a cross-functional partner version, and a customer-facing safe version. Same truth, different framing. That is how your story travels. You can also use AI to automate the storyboard habit. Create a simple template in a doc, and every week paste in the latest Amplitude or Mixpanel snapshot. Ask AI to fill the storyboard sections; then you edit for accuracy. This is not laziness. This is leverage. It keeps your updates consistent, and it reduces the emotional labor of translating messy metrics over and over again. If you are using Pendo, you can go one step further and connect the story to action. When you see a weak activation step in the funnel, you can immediately pair it with an in-app guide or tooltip. Then the story is not just "here is the data." The story becomes "here is the data and here is the intervention." That is what makes leadership trust you even when numbers are still warming up.

The Data Storyboard Canvas

To make this repeatable, you can use a very simple canvas each time you prepare a post-launch story.

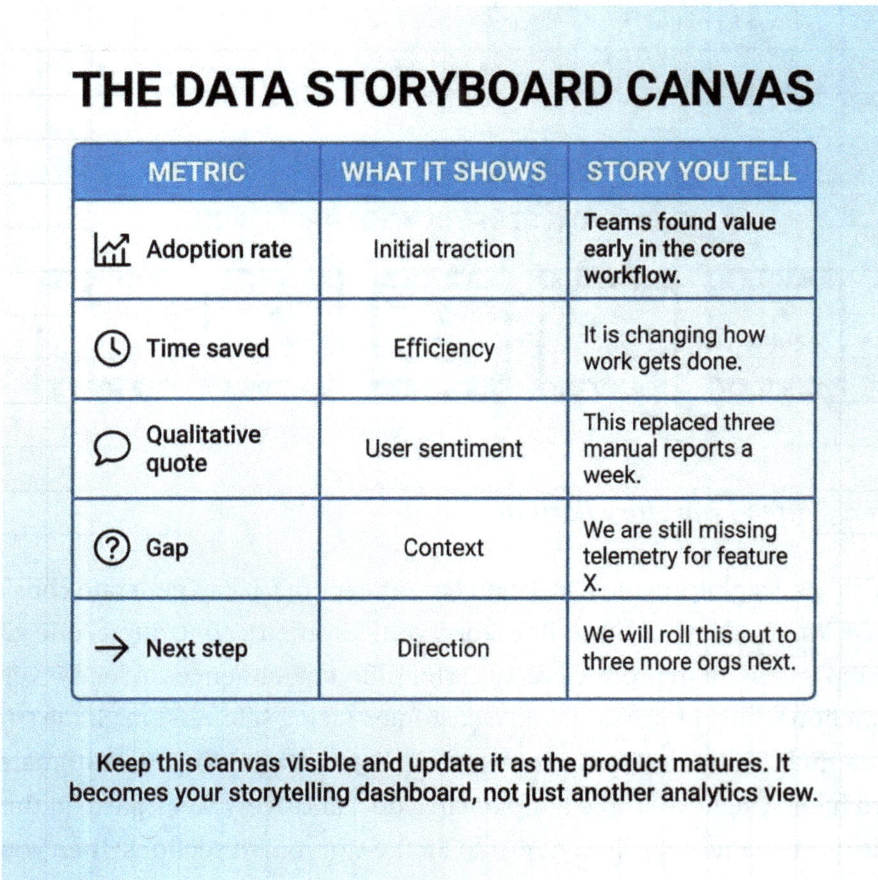

THE DATA STORYBOARD CANVAS

METRIC	WHAT IT SHOWS	STORY YOU TELL
Adoption rate	Initial traction	Teams found value early in the core workflow.
Time saved	Efficiency	It is changing how work gets done.
Qualitative quote	User sentiment	This replaced three manual reports a week.
Gap	Context	We are still missing telemetry for feature X.
Next step	Direction	We will roll this out to three more orgs next.

Keep this canvas visible and update it as the product matures. It becomes your storytelling dashboard, not just another analytics view.

Figure 7-3. *Metrics-to-Story Canvas*

You keep this canvas small enough that you can fill it in quickly, but rich enough that it forces you to look beyond one or two vanity charts. You keep it visible and you update it as the product matures. It becomes your storytelling dashboard, not just another analytics view.

You do not need a fancy tool for this. A simple table in a doc that you revisit for every feature or phase is enough. The habit is what matters.

The Data Storytelling Playbook

At this point, you have the pieces. Anchor every metric in the business outcome it supports. Define your success signals before you ship. Pair every number with a story that explains the behavior behind it. Be transparent about gaps so people trust the parts that are solid. Package your updates as small, repeatable narratives anyone can carry into their own rooms.

The underlying truth is simple. You are not in the business of spinning data. You are in the business of translating learning.

Credibility is the invisible currency of enterprise product management. You earn a little more of it every time you stand in front of imperfect charts, tell the truth calmly, and still make a clear case for what you are learning and where you are going next.

The Data Storytelling Playbook

[illegible]

CHAPTER 8

Scaling the Platform: From V1 to Vn

Building the V1 of a product is like laying the first stone of a cathedral. It is ambitious, a little idealistic, and just enough to prove that something beautiful could exist there one day.

Scaling that same thing into a robust, boring in a good way, self-sustaining platform that delivers value across multiple user groups, use cases, or geographies is a very different game. V1 is about proof. Vn is about permanence. V1 is "this works." Vn is "this is how people use this every day."

That shift requires discipline, architectural foresight, and a deep understanding of how your organization and your users actually behave when nobody is looking. Scaling is not just about growing. It is about growing with purpose and resilience and not setting yourself up to spend the next two years apologizing for outages in leadership reviews.

In this chapter, we unpack what it really means to move from a validated V1 to a scaled platform. We cover technical readiness, change management, platform evangelism, governance models, and the cultural shifts you need if you want the thing you built to last longer than your current reorg cycle and actually stick with users.

© Anusha Ravi and Nitika Malhotra 2026
A. Ravi and N. Malhotra, *Launching Enterprise Products*, https://doi.org/10.1007/979-8-8688-2661-0_8

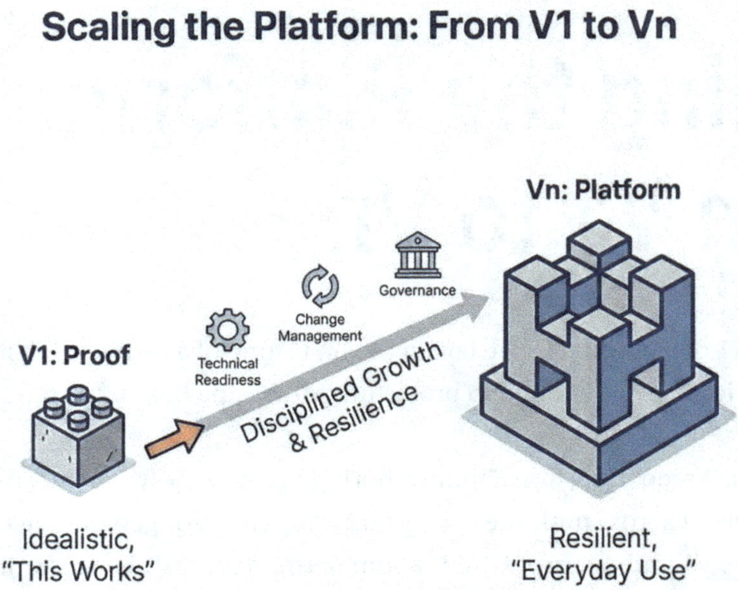

Figure 8-1. *Scaling the Platform*

Start by Stabilizing the Foundation

Your V1 was built to prove that the product delivers value. Full stop. It probably carries technical debt, manual workflows, half-documented decisions, and at least one "temporary" integration that everyone quietly agreed not to talk about. That is normal.

What is not normal is trying to scale that V1 as is. If you skip the stabilization step, you are basically building a tower on sand and then acting surprised when the first real storm hits.

So before you race to add more users, more high-value accounts, more regions, and more features, you pause. You invest in stabilizing the thing you already have.

You start with reliability. You pay down technical debt on the most brittle paths. You clean up the code paths that only pass tests because someone added a retry loop at 2 a.m. during launch week. Performance bottlenecks that were tolerable in pilot mode with 20 users will absolutely break at scale when 2,000 users log in on Monday morning. That one API that was "fine" for a handful of internal users will not be fine when multiple external customers hit it at once.

Then you think about modularity. You look at what you shipped and ask, "What here needs to be core and what can sit on the edges." You break monoliths into services or reusable modules wherever it makes sense. You make it possible for different user-facing experiences to evolve without rewriting your core spine. You design for flexibility in deployment, not just "whatever works on dev right now."

You also instrument everything. You cannot scale what you cannot see. Observability is not a nice to have at this stage; it is survival. You add logs, metrics, and dashboards that speak to product health and user experience, not just system uptime. You make it easy for anyone on the team to answer simple questions like "Are new users seeing slow page loads?" or "Are a few large customers driving all the traffic?" without needing a 4-hour war room.

Data maturity becomes part of your foundation too. You build the pipelines, models, and access layers that downstream consumers will rely on when they start using your data at scale. That includes access controls so not every person can query production tables, lineage so you know where data came from, versioning so changes do not silently break reporting, and privacy baked in from day one.

And then documentation. Documentation becomes a first-class citizen instead of an afterthought. A stable foundation is one others can build on, and that does not just mean code. You need technical documentation, onboarding playbooks, and design rationales that explain why things are the way they are. You are not writing a novel. You are giving future you and future contributors a map.

The goal here is not perfection. The goal is predictability. Ask yourself a few simple questions. Can this thing handle 10x usage without waking up half the team at night? Can you onboard the next few hundred users or a new large client without breaking everything they touch? Can you debug the most common issues without needing the one original engineer who has mentally moved on? If the answer is no to any of those, you are not ready to scale.

You see this play out all the time in enterprise SaaS. A workflow automation tool gets built for a specific internal group of power users in one geography. It works beautifully. A small set of users relies on it every day. Then sales lands a large customer who wants the same experience, and suddenly you have thousands of users hitting the system. Latency spikes, jobs back up, and what used to be a "hero moment" for the team becomes a weekly incident review. The problem was not that the product was bad. The problem was that the foundation was never stabilized before usage expanded.

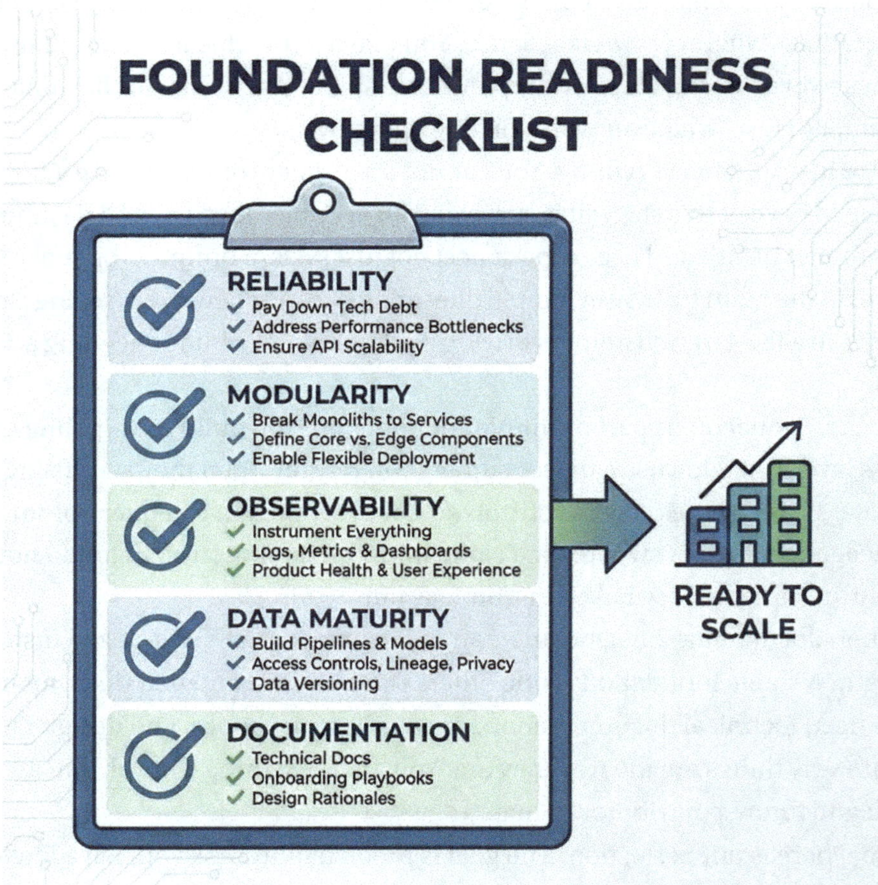

Figure 8-2. *Foundation Readiness Checklist*

How to leverage AI in foundation stabilization and what tools actually help: This is one of the highest-leverage places to use AI, because stabilization work is often buried under tribal knowledge. AI helps you surface patterns, prioritize debt, and shorten incident recovery. Start with technical debt triage. Feed your bug backlog, incident summaries, and top support tickets into an AI assistant and ask it to cluster them into brittle paths, performance hotspots, integration risk, and developer experience pain. You will usually find that 20% of your platform causes 80% of the operational pain. That becomes your stabilization roadmap, not a random list of chores.

Create an entire agentic workflow to streamline your process. Use AI for observability and incident learning, because scaling creates noise and humans miss patterns. Tools like Datadog, New Relic, Splunk, Grafana, and Sentry can give you logs and traces, but the real win is faster interpretation. Many of these tools now have AI-assisted detection and summarization capabilities that help you spot anomalies, probable root causes, and blast radius without a 4-hour war room. Pair that with PagerDuty or Opsgenie for incident response, and you can turn a messy outage into a clean post-incident narrative in minutes, not days. Use AI for documentation so you stop relying on the one engineer who remembers everything. If you have code and architecture decisions scattered across tickets and docs, use an AI assistant to generate a first draft of system overviews, runbooks, and onboarding guides, then have the team review for correctness. Good homes for this are Confluence, Notion, GitBook, or a docs site like Docusaurus.

The goal is not pretty docs. The goal is searchable institutional memory. For modularity and API stability, the right tools matter. Use API gateways and management tools like Apigee, Kong, or AWS API Gateway so you can enforce policies and versioning. Use feature flags like LaunchDarkly so you can ship safely and roll back without panic. Use CI and quality gates with tools like GitHub Actions, GitLab CI, and SonarQube, and if your org allows it, GitHub Copilot for faster refactors and test coverage expansion. AI does not replace engineering judgment, but it absolutely helps you move through the boring work faster, which is exactly what scaling requires.

Treat Adoption As a Product

Now for the part that is both annoying and true. Just because the platform works does not mean people will use it. Adoption, especially when you are asking users to change their workflows, does not magically happen. It needs to be owned and designed deliberately.

You have to treat adoption with the same rigor that you would use for a new feature launch to external customers. Inside your own company or in your customer base, you effectively have a go-to-market motion, even if nobody calls it that.

You start by creating clear value stories for different stakeholder types. What you say to an IC engineer is not what you say to a VP. An engineer might care that your platform gives them clean APIs and removes three integration steps. A frontline manager might care that their team now spends less time in spreadsheets. A VP might only care that this platform unlocks a long-term strategy line item on a 3-year plan. The pain you are solving has to be framed in their language, not yours.

You lower the barrier to entry for users. That means providing quick start experiences that are actually quick, not a 40-page PDF. It might mean product tours, contextual hints, or templates that users can start from instead of staring at an empty state. It might mean sample workspaces, demo accounts, or sandboxes where users can click around without the fear of breaking something important. First, use should feel like "Oh, this is helpful," not like "I need a 3-hour training for this."

You think land and expand instead of "big-bang rollout." You identify your early users and power users, the ones who feel the pain the most and are open to trying new tools. You support their early use cases deeply and make sure they get to an actual outcome, not just a login. Then you leverage their success to pull in others. Grassroots adoption among users is underrated. A single enthusiastic power user can bring in a team. A team can influence a whole function.

You design your adoption loops so that usage gets rewarded in visible ways. You surface metrics that show time saved, reduced manual work, fewer errors, or faster decision cycles. You do not just say "please use this." You show that "users who adopt this flow resolve tasks 30% faster," and suddenly everyone wants that.

You remember that different user personas have different needs and levels of comfort with complexity. A data scientist may want deep controls and flexibility. A business manager may want opinionated defaults and simple configuration. You design the platform so it can serve both without becoming unusable for either. You avoid building something that is perfect for your most technical users and incomprehensible for everyone else.

Adoption is not a one-time event that happens after launch and then you move on. It is an ongoing cycle of communication, feedback, and iteration. Scaling a platform without a user adoption plan is a classic enterprise miss. People assume the value will sell itself. It rarely does.

Think of an internal experimentation platform inside a large consumer app company. V1 lets one growth team ship A/B tests faster. It is a win. Then individual PMs in other groups start to hear about it. Then marketing wants to run campaigns through it.

Then product analytics wants to standardize all experiments on that platform. The teams that treat adoption like a product build intuitive UIs, clear user docs, office hours, and internal stories around specific user wins. The teams that do not end up with five separate testing tools, confused users, and no single source of truth are the ones that are struggling.

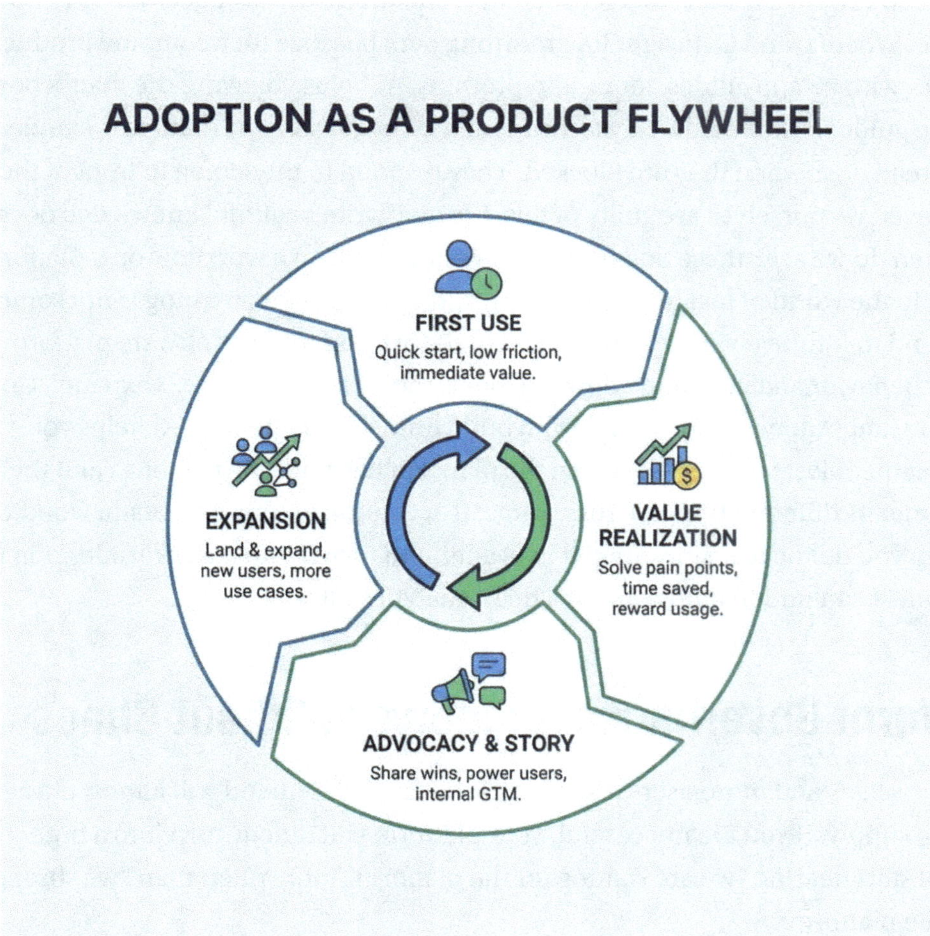

***Figure 8-3.** Adoption As a Product Flywheel*

How to leverage AI for adoption and the tools that make it easier: AI helps you scale adoption work without turning the PM into a full-time enablement person. And do we know the pain of this? How often do PMs have to jump between CS, CX, Sales, and Marketing to help smoothen out narratives due to minor misalignments in shared understanding? This is where we can use AI to generate persona-specific value narratives fast. One story for builders, one story for operators, one story for leaders. Same platform, different language.

This is where you can use ChatGPT or Gemini to draft talk tracks, training snippets, and launch posts, and then you edit them to match your org tone and reality. For in-product adoption, use tools that let you intervene where the user gets stuck. Pendo, WalkMe, Whatfix, and Gainsight PX are strong here because they combine product analytics with in-app guides, tours, and prompts. AI helps you write the microcopy, propose guide flows, and quickly test variations. The reason this matters is simple. Users do not read docs when they are blocked. They respond to the screen in front of them. I mean, even we ourselves are guilty of this. We may write beautiful knowledge docs, but how often do we seek these docs out when we are stuck on a workflow on a platform? We live in the world of instant gratification, and searching for anything is not something users tend to intuitively do or want the mental workload for in a software platform.

For behavior analytics and adoption loops, tools like Amplitude, Mixpanel, Google Analytics, and Adobe Analytics help you build funnels and cohorts. AI helps you interpret them faster, especially when the platform has multiple personas and the same metric means different things across teams. If activation is "first successful workflow," AI can help you define it cleanly, map it to events, and turn it into a weekly adoption pulse that leaders can understand without a deep analytics tutorial.

Platform Governance: Empower Without Chaos

As usage scales and more users discover your platform, demand will almost always outpace supply. If you are not careful, your platform will quietly turn into a bottleneck. You will start hearing "we are waiting for the platform" more often than "we shipped using the platform."

Governance models exist to guard against that, but they can easily turn into bureaucracy if you are not careful. The job is to enable users and product teams to move fast with guardrails, not to slow everyone down in the name of control.

One useful pattern is a decentralized contribution model. You let trusted contributors extend the platform within clear guardrails. In a SaaS context, this might look like advanced users or partner teams building integrations or extensions using your public APIs and extension points. Inside an enterprise, it might look like domain teams contributing new connectors or templates. Think of it like open source inside your company or ecosystem. The core team controls the vision, contracts, and base quality bar. Other contributors can build on top as long as they follow the standards. This not only increases capacity but also builds a sense of shared ownership among your user base.

You lean into APIs over gatekeeping. Wherever possible, you provide self-service capabilities instead of "submit a request and wait for three weeks." If users or downstream teams can safely help themselves, they will. If every integration or new use case requires a meeting with your team, they will route around you or get frustrated and go back to their old tools.

You are intentional about versioning and deprecation policies. Backward compatibility is boring to talk about until you break a key workflow for hundreds of users because you removed a field they relied on. You define how versions are rolled out, how long they live, and how you communicate deprecations. You avoid breaking changes unless they are absolutely necessary, and when you do need one, you plan it like a small product launch, with clear user impact and migration paths.

You might use a change advisory board or smaller working groups. Not as gatekeepers that kill ideas in committee, but as forums for roadmap alignment and feedback loops. These groups can represent different user segments or internal systems that rely on your platform. They help surface conflicts early and create transparency, instead of everyone discovering the conflict at launch.

You also define SLAs and SLOs. Users need to know what they can depend on. Is this platform "best effort," or is it part of their business-critical workflow? If your platform is on the golden path for other products and user workflows, they need confidence that when something breaks, you are on it. Reliability is as much about expectations as it is about uptime.

Done well, platform governance becomes a flywheel. Every new use case strengthens the core. Every serious user becomes a more informed user. Your platform becomes not just stable, but sustainable.

You see this in internal developer platforms or data platforms at many large SaaS companies. The ones that win user hearts do not hoard all the build work. They define standards, offer paved paths, give users clear APIs, and let advanced users extend the platform responsibly. Over time, "using the platform" becomes the fastest, safest way for users and teams to achieve what they want, not the slowest.

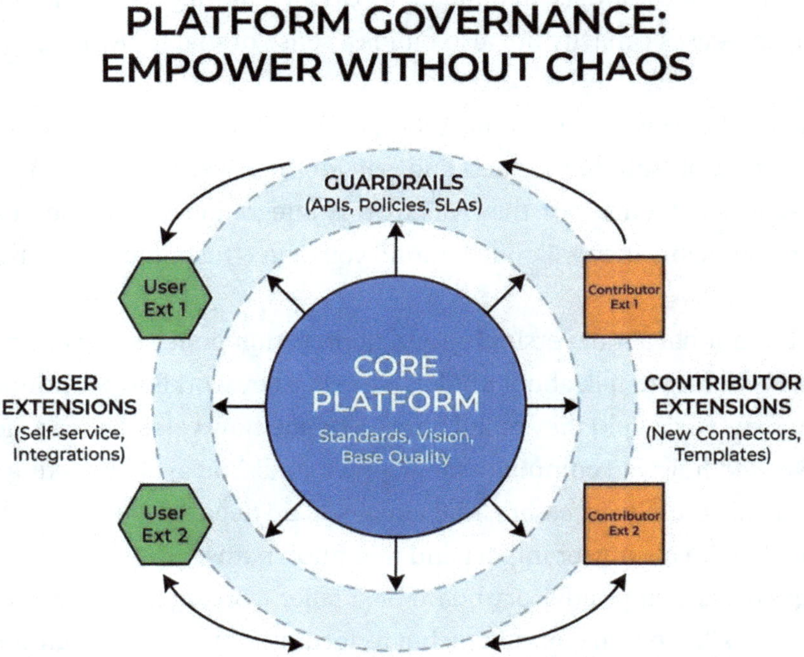

Figure 8-4. *Platform Governance Model*

How to leverage AI for governance without creating bureaucracy and the tools that help: Governance usually fails when it becomes manual and political. AI helps you make governance more structured and less personal. Start with intake. Use AI to summarize incoming requests, detect duplicates, map them to your platform charter, and propose an initial severity and repeatability score. This is where tools like Jira Product Discovery, Productboard, Aha!, Linear, or even a well-structured form feeding into a backlog can work well, because the discipline matters more than the brand. AI just makes the triage faster and more consistent. For decentralized contribution models, the right tooling reduces chaos. Use GitHub or GitLab for contribution workflows, CODEOWNERS for review boundaries, automated checks for quality, and templated pull requests for extensions and connectors.

AI can draft contribution guidelines, generate scaffolding for new connectors, and speed up code review summaries, but your standards still drive the quality bar. For versioning and deprecation, use API management tooling like Apigee or Kong, documentation portals like GitBook or a docs site, and automated comms triggers for deprecation notices. AI can help you write deprecation notices that are clear, migration guides that are step by step, and release notes that match different audiences. This is how you keep governance firm without being annoying.

Invest in Platform Evangelism

Adoption and governance are necessary, but they are not enough. If you want your platform to scale, you also need narrative scale. Someone has to tell the story of why this platform exists and why it matters now, in a way that resonates with actual users. That is where evangelism comes in.

Evangelism is not about hype. It is about building momentum.

You start by branding the platform. Give it a name that users can say without tripping over acronyms. Give it a simple identity, a mark, a color, something that makes it recognizable in release notes or dashboards. Give it a home, usually an internal microsite or external docs site that acts as the single source of truth for it. When users ask "where do I go to learn about this," the answer should not be "ask whoever built it three years ago."

You tell stories. You document user wins and spotlight them in newsletters, internal feeds, customer webinars, all hands, and leadership reviews. Peer validation is more persuasive than a hundred PM decks. When another product area hears "users who switched to this platform flow cut their reporting time in half," they pay attention. When a customer sees a case study that sounds like their own problem and sees real numbers, they lean in.

You create rituals. Maybe it is monthly platform updates. Maybe it is office hours. Maybe it is user groups and demo days where users and builders show their favorite workflows, automations, or integrations on top of your platform. Community builds culture. Rituals keep that culture alive.

You build feedback loops into the way you evangelize. You share a roadmap and invite input. You close the loop when users give feedback and you act on it, or even when you do not act and explain why. When users feel heard, they stay engaged even when things are not perfect. You make it very obvious how users can suggest improvements, report issues, or propose new use cases.

And you show impact. You quantify and communicate business value consistently. Not just vanity metrics like "number of accounts enabled," but outcomes. How much effort did users save? How many manual reports went away. How many incidents were avoided? How many decisions got faster or more accurate? You keep laying out the receipts.

You are not just building a product at this point. You are building a movement. The platform should feel like the future of how users will work, not just another option they can ignore. People want to be part of that future.

Think of how internal data query platforms or self-serve analytics tools grew inside large SaaS companies. The ones that won were the ones whose PMs and tech leads treated the platform like a user product with a story. They named it, showed up at every internal forum with real user stories, made it easy for non technical users to onboard, and kept showing "before vs. after" in real workflows. Suddenly, not using the platform looked like being stuck in the stone age.

How to leverage AI for evangelism and recommended tools for narrative scale: Evangelism gets easier when you can package wins quickly and consistently. Use AI to turn raw inputs into shareable artifacts. One customer quote plus one metric plus one screenshot becomes a Slack post, a newsletter blurb, a 1-minute talk track, and a two-slide leadership update. Same truth, different packaging. That is how the story travels when you are not in the room.

For the actual distribution, use whatever channels your org already trusts. A docs hub in Confluence, Notion, GitBook, or SharePoint. A regular update in Slack or Teams. A monthly deck in Google Slides or PowerPoint. A short internal video if your company culture responds to that. AI helps you draft, summarize, and keep the message consistent, but the ritual is what creates momentum. If your platform has a lot of user questions, use AI-powered support flows so the team does not drown. Tools like Zendesk, Intercom, or Jira Service Management can help structure intake and knowledge base linking. AI can summarize tickets, suggest knowledge articles, and reduce repeat questions, which frees you up to do real platform work instead of repeating the same explanation 200 times.

Know When to Say No

Every platform that shows even a hint of success becomes a magnet for requests. Users, customer-facing teams, and leaders will all have ideas. Some of these will be very valid and very urgent. Some of them will be "Can you also make it do this completely unrelated thing by the end of quarter?" If you say yes to everything, you dilute platform quality and lose your north star.

Guarding that north star is part of your job.

You start by defining your platform charter clearly. What user problems will this platform solve? What is out of scope for the next 12 to 24 months? You revisit and socialize this often because enterprise memory is short and orgs change. When a shiny new request shows up, you can point back to the charter and have a grounding conversation, instead of debating from scratch every time.

You create intake frameworks. You do not need a 40-page scoring model, but you do need a simple way to compare requests. You look at expected impact, alignment to long-term strategy, and repeatability across users and accounts. You ask, "If we build this, will many users and customers benefit, or is this essentially a custom one-off." You try to be data-driven about what gets prioritized, even if the data is directional.

You define escalation paths. If someone really believes their request should be an exception, give them a way to make that case without needing to escalate in ten different directions. This keeps flexibility without turning everything into ad hoc lobbying.

You also build cultural discipline inside your own team. You teach your team that "no" is not negative. It is protective. Protective of the mission. Protective of the experience. Protective of the users and customers that already rely on the platform. You normalize saying, "Not now" or "This belongs in a different system" instead of bending the platform to become whatever the loudest stakeholder wants this week.

Scaling responsibly means drawing boundaries strategically, transparently, and without ego. It means choosing what not to do and having the discipline to stick to it, even when sponsorship pressure shows up.

There is always that moment where a senior leader asks for something that technically could be done on your platform but would pull you far away from your core user problems. The easy answer is yes. The right answer is often a thoughtful no, with a clear explanation of why you are protecting the platform and how you can still support the underlying business goal in another way.

How to leverage AI to say no cleanly without burning relationships: AI helps you turn "no" into clarity instead of conflict. Use it to generate a response that includes three things: the request summary in neutral language, the reason it is out of scope tied back to the charter, and an alternative path that still supports the underlying goal. This is especially useful when you are replying to senior stakeholders and you want to sound firm but not defensive. You can also use AI to keep your intake scoring consistent.

When every request is triaged through the same lens, you stop debating each one like a brand new moral crisis. Tools like Jira Product Discovery, Productboard, or even a structured spreadsheet work well here. The key is that the framework is visible and repeatable, and AI just makes the mechanics faster.

Signs You Are Scaling Right

So how do you know your platform is actually scaling well and you are not just busy?

You should start seeing new users and new accounts onboard themselves with very little friction. They might still ask the occasional question, but they are not stuck waiting for you at every step. They find the docs, follow the paved path, and get to value without needing a personal escort.

You should see your platform's NPS or equivalent sentiment from users improve over time. That does not mean everyone is thrilled all the time. It does mean that as you stabilize, govern, and evangelize, the overall experience feels better and more reliable to the people using it.

You notice that feature requests increasingly come with concrete context or contributions. Power users might propose configurations, small extensions, or even code changes if that is part of your model. Users are not just asking you to build everything. They want to co-create and extend the platform within the guardrails you set. That is a sign of healthy ownership and engagement.

You see users and products building on top of your APIs instead of around them. You hear fewer stories of "we built our own workaround because yours was too hard to work with" and more stories of "we just plugged into the platform and got what we needed."

Inside your own team, you see more time spent on strategic improvements and less on basic support tickets and user firefighting. You are not spending every day doing reactive triage. You actually have breathing room to think about where the platform should go next and how to better serve your users.

You start getting pulled into strategic planning conversations by leadership, not just tactical project reviews. People see the platform as an enabler of big bets that will touch thousands or millions of users, not just a utility that keeps the lights on.

In the best case, the platform eventually becomes the default way of working for the users and customers it touches. New products assume they will sit on top of it. New user-facing features assume they will integrate with it. Doing things any other way starts to look strange. That is when you know you have moved from V1 proof to Vn permanence.

Scaling a platform is the art of building both the product and the community around it. It is equal parts engineering, storytelling, advocacy, and leadership. If you do it right, your product stops being "a tool that one group built" and starts being the invisible operating system of how users work across your organization or ecosystem.

A simple tool stack recommendation for this chapter so you can actually execute V1 to Vn

1. **For Reliability, Observability, and Incidents**: Datadog or New Relic for monitoring, Splunk or Elastic for logs if your org is heavy on log search, Grafana if you want flexible dashboards, Sentry for application errors, and PagerDuty or Opsgenie for on-call and incident workflows.

2. **For Product and Adoption Analytics**: Amplitude or Mixpanel for funnels and retention, Google Analytics or Adobe Analytics if your org standardizes on them, and Pendo or WalkMe for in-product guides plus behavioral insight.

3. **For Platform Documentation and Enablement**: Confluence, Notion, GitBook, or a docs site like Docusaurus, plus a consistent release notes channel in Slack or Teams.

4. **For Governance and Intake**: Jira Product Discovery or Productboard for a structured request pipeline, GitHub or GitLab for contribution workflows, and LaunchDarkly for safe rollout controls.

5. **For AI Leverage Across All of It**: Use an AI assistant for synthesis and packaging, plus the AI capabilities embedded in your observability and adoption tools to reduce noise and speed up interpretation. The goal is not to chase shiny tools. The goal is to make scaling boring in a good way.

The goal is not to chase shiny tools. The goal is to make scaling boring in a good way.

Next up, we explore how to navigate reorgs, leadership shifts, and the inevitable change that comes when your product succeeds beyond its initial home. Because once your platform matters, the org will absolutely move around it, and you will need a whole new set of skills to keep your momentum alive.

CHAPTER 9

Navigating Org Change and Reorgs

If you build something impactful, the organization will eventually rearrange itself around it, on top of it, or straight through it. Sometimes in support of your work. Sometimes despite it. Sometimes because of it.

Reorgs are not rare in enterprise. They are the default. Leadership will keep shifting scope, reporting lines, and priorities for strategy, costs, risk, and personalities. Your job is not to avoid org change. Your job is to build products that live through it.

In this chapter, we look at how to anticipate reorgs without becoming paranoid, how to protect your product's momentum when the boxes and lines move, and how to occasionally use structural change as an accelerant instead of a setback.

© Anusha Ravi and Nitika Malhotra 2026
A. Ravi and N. Malhotra, *Launching Enterprise Products*, https://doi.org/10.1007/979-8-8688-2661-0_9

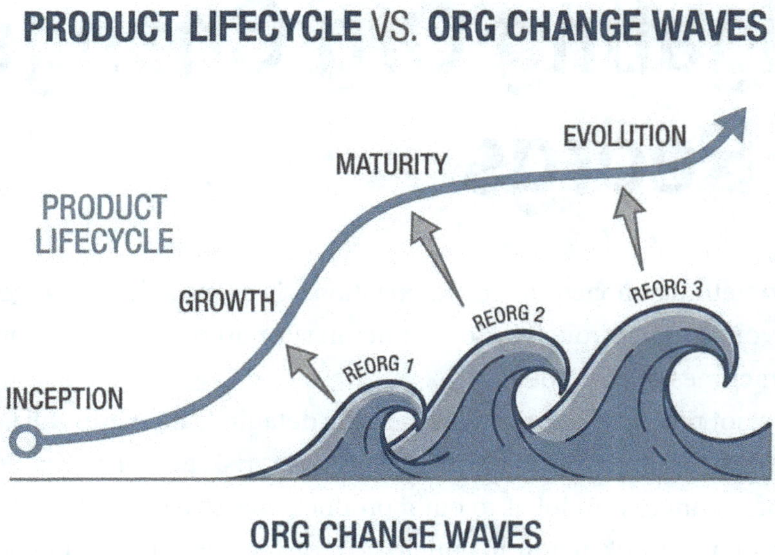

Figure 9-1. *Product Lifecycle vs. Org Change Waves*

Anchor to Business Value, Not Org Structure

The products that survive multiple reorgs are not the ones with the prettiest diagrams. They are the ones whose value is unmistakably tied to real outcomes. Those products are not overcoupled to a single sponsor, a single team, or a specific reporting line that can vanish in one leadership shuffle.

Start by being brutally clear about why your product exists. If someone asked you in a hallway, could you explain the business outcomes it drives in one or two sentences, without opening a slide? If the only thing you can talk about is features or technical elegance, you are vulnerable. You want language like, "This platform cuts partner onboarding time from three weeks to three days" or "This tool reduces invoice errors and saves measurable revenue every quarter."

Then make sure that value is not locked inside one narrow lane. A product that only one function touches is easy to sunset when that function gets rebranded or merged. A product that several functions rely on is hard to kill quietly. You want people in Operations, Engineering, Analytics, Finance, Marketing, or Support all able to say, "If you remove this, my work gets harder and outcomes get worse." That is armor.

Look for ways your product can live beyond your immediate org boundary. If it is a seller tool, can it show up in partner materials? If it is an internal platform, can it support use cases in multiple business units, regions, or lines of business? When your product has visible usage outside your home box on the org chart, it picks up resilience. Even if your team moves, what you built is now part of someone else's critical path.

Value stories become your long-term memory. Leadership will change. Your reporting line will change. The reorg email will land at 5:32 p.m. on a Thursday. What should not change is the story of what your product has done. Keep that story alive in short write-ups, before-and-after metrics, and real user quotes. These are the artifacts that outlast the people.

There is a reason some internal platforms become "too useful to kill." In one large SaaS company, an internal experimentation platform started as a side project inside a growth team. Over a few years, it became the standard way to run tests across multiple product lines because everyone could point to clear results: higher conversion, faster learning, and fewer one-off analytics requests. When a reorg moved the original team, leadership briefly considered replacing the platform with something external. The idea died as soon as they saw the impact metrics and heard how many teams and PMs depended on it. Business value, not politics, kept it alive.

A product that is rooted in outcomes will always outlast the current org chart. Build something meaningfully important and keep its value decoupled not just from the product metrics but from any single organizational configuration.

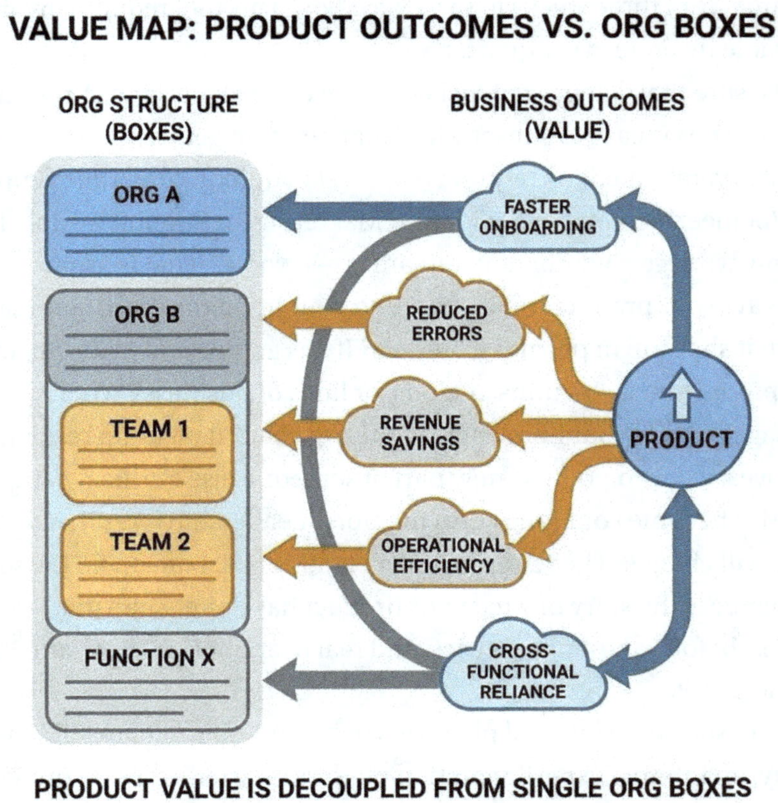

Figure 9-2. *Value Map: Product Outcomes vs. Org Boxes*

AI is useful here because reorgs create narrative chaos. Everyone has their own version of what matters and why. The fastest way to stay grounded is to keep your value story short, consistent, and repeatable. Use an AI assistant to help you distill your product into two sentences, one outcome statement and one proof statement. Outcome is what it changes. Proof is the metric or artifact that backs it. Then you test it. If a leader can repeat it without your slide deck, it is working. If they cannot, it needs tightening. AI can also help you generate variations of the value story by audience. Same product, different lens. For example, for finance leaders it is cost and efficiency. For engineering leaders it is reliability and reduced integration complexity. For operations it is cycle time and fewer escalations. You do not change the truth. You change the translation. This is how you make your product value legible across org boundaries, which is the real protection in a reorg.

Build Multi-Threaded Relationships

When reorgs land, single-threaded dependencies are a liability. If only one leader understands your product, one champion cares about it, or one team keeps the lights on, your fate is tied to whatever happens to that one thread.

You protect your product by spreading context and ownership on purpose.

Redundancy in relationships is a feature, not waste. Build relationships with more than one executive. Get more than one senior manager excited about the outcomes. Share regular updates with more than one peer group. This is not politics for the sake of politics. It is risk management. If one person leaves, gets rescoped, or simply has a new priority, you are not starting from zero.

Invest in peer alliances. Create a coalition of people whose work clearly benefits from your product. That might be other PMs who build on your APIs, data leads who rely on your exports, or frontline managers whose teams are more effective because of your tools. If enough people care and feel ownership, someone will fight for the product when the org is reshuffled.

Leadership narratives matter too. Do not wait until your VP is leaving to remember their peers have never heard of your product. Periodically share product updates and value stories in broader forums. Join staff meetings when invited. Offer short segments in internal town halls or business reviews. Every time you frame the narrative at that level, you are teaching more senior people how to talk about your work in rooms you are not in.

Documentation is part of relationship building. It is not just for engineers. Make sure the story of "why this exists" and "what this enables" is written down somewhere that a new leader could read and absorb without a guided tour. If the product only truly lives in a few heads, it leaves when those heads move. Spread the load, in both human and written form.

You can see the cost of single-threaded influence when a beloved internal customization lives only in the mind of one admin. The day that person leaves or gets reassigned, nobody knows how it works. Then the reorg hits, and a new leader looks at this mysterious dependency with no advocates and says, "We can probably replace this." Multithreaded relationships and clear artifacts would have been cheaper.

The hard part about multithreading is not intention. It is time and consistency. AI helps you package and distribute context without writing everything from scratch. Use AI to convert one core update into multiple formats: a short Slack note, a one-slide summary, a three-sentence exec update, and a longer doc version. Then you share the right version in the right forum. This is how you keep more than one leader informed without living inside status updates. AI also helps you map relationships. Take your stakeholder list and ask an AI assistant to categorize them into decision makers, influencers, implementers, and users, and then identify where you are single-threaded. You will usually find one or two critical gaps, like you have engineering but not finance, or you have ops but not security. Then you make intentional moves to fill those gaps before the org chart forces you to.

Reposition, Not Resist

It is very tempting to fight a reorg. To argue your way out of a move. To refuse a new scope. To escalate against a change you do not like. Sometimes that is justified. Most of the time, outright resistance burns social capital without changing the outcome.

Instead of digging in your heels, treat reorgs as a moment to reposition. This happens all too often, and change is the only constant in the product world; the more skilled you are at this, the better you will be able to navigate the changes. Nobody wants to be remembered as the person who was too difficult during an already challenging and changing landscape. We want to be the person that is storytelling under pressure.

AI helps you move faster without saying something sloppy. The moment a reorg hits, use AI to draft a repositioning brief with four sections: what changed, what stayed the same, what new opportunity exists, and what you need to deliver value under the new structure. Then you use that brief to walk into the first meeting with a new leader calm and prepared. AI is also helpful in finding the overlap story. When two teams merge and tools overlap, you want to be the team that can say, "Here is the consolidation plan and here is what we can retire." Take the list of existing tools and workflows and have AI help you compare them by users, capabilities, and outcomes. Then you propose a migration path. The team that brings a clean plan becomes the team that gets trusted.

Start with a simple question. "What new opportunity just opened up?" A different leader might have a mandate that aligns better with what your product can do. A new structure might connect you more directly to the decision-makers or users who benefit most. A merge between business units might expose overlapping tools that your platform can replace. If you only see the loss, you will miss the openings.

Offer your platform as part of the solution. Reorgs have a way of exposing duplicative efforts that everyone knew about but nobody had a clean way to fix. If you can show that your product consolidates three separate tools, simplifies workflows, or gives leadership a single source of truth, you move from "team that is being moved" to "team that solves a problem created by this reorg."

Use the disruption to reset narratives. Org changes are often the only time when people are actively open to reframing scope, charters, and boundaries. This is your chance to clarify what your product is and is not, to sharpen positioning, to say no to legacy responsibilities that no longer make sense, and to tackle technical debt that has been hard to prioritize. "While we are restructuring" is surprisingly effective cover for cleanup that helps you scale later.

Stay outcome-focused. When people are stressed and confused, conversations drift into fear. Your job is to keep bringing it back to results. Show up with metrics, customer stories, and clear value. Say, "Here is what this platform is doing for users and revenue. Here is how we can help with the new priorities." Emotions are human. They are not a strategy.

Senior product leaders who thrive through reorgs are not the ones who never get moved. They are the ones who know how to absorb change, reposition their product, and use the new structure to unlock scale they could not reach before.

A simple example. A data reporting tool started inside Finance. A cost-cutting reorg moved it under a centralized analytics function. The PM could have fought to stay in finance, where the relationships were comfortable. Instead, they leaned into the change, pitched the tool as the standard reporting platform across multiple functions, and used the moment to get scope and resourcing to support more users. Resistance would have kept them small. Repositioning made them central.

Create Organizational Memory

The easiest way to future-proof a product is to make sure it can tell its own story when you are not in the room. That means building organizational memory on purpose.

Think about what an inheriting leader or acquiring team would need to see to understand why your product matters. Internal case studies and short impact briefs are a good start. Take one user group or customer and show clearly what changed before and after your product. Focus on the real work, not just the UI.

Architecture diagrams and data flow maps matter too, but keep them at the right altitude. You want artifacts that explain, "Here is how this fits into our ecosystem and what depends on it," not fifty tiny boxes in unreadable font. Someone should be able to glance at it and understand the dependency graph.

Time series adoption metrics are powerful. Show usage over time, segmented by user types or cohorts. Show stickiness, not just signups. Show how usage behaves through org changes or new product launches. These curves tell a story about durability.

Testimonials from internal users or external customers add weight. Screenshots of comments, short quotes, and little anecdotes like "This saved me three hours every week" are small but memorable. A skeptical new leader is more likely to believe the voice of a peer user than a generic claim from a PM.

AI is a cheat code for turning scattered artifacts into a coherent memory system. Most teams already have the raw material: meeting notes, tickets, design docs, PRDs, release notes, incident writeups, and random threads. The problem is that it is not packaged in a way a new leader can consume. Use AI to produce a small set of canonical artifacts and keep them updated. A practical workflow is to maintain a living product brief and a living impact brief. Every month, you paste the latest updates and metrics into an AI assistant and ask it to refresh the brief while keeping it concise. Then a human does a quick review for accuracy. Over time, the product can speak for itself because the artifacts stay current. Tools matter here. Use a knowledge base like Confluence or Notion as the home. Use Google Drive for simple, shareable briefs. Use a slide deck template for the exec pitch. If your org uses an internal wiki or docs portal, publish there. The point is not to create more docs. The point is to make the right small set of docs impossible to ignore.

Create a short "pitch deck" for execs who may inherit your product or your team. It should answer the basics. What is this? Who uses it? What value does it drive? What is next? What would break if we removed it? This is not for fundraising. It is for survival.

If your product had to be repitched tomorrow with none of the original team in the room, could it stand on its own? Would the artifacts and usage speak clearly enough? If the answer is no, start building that memory now. Waiting until a reorg forces your hand is a bad plan.

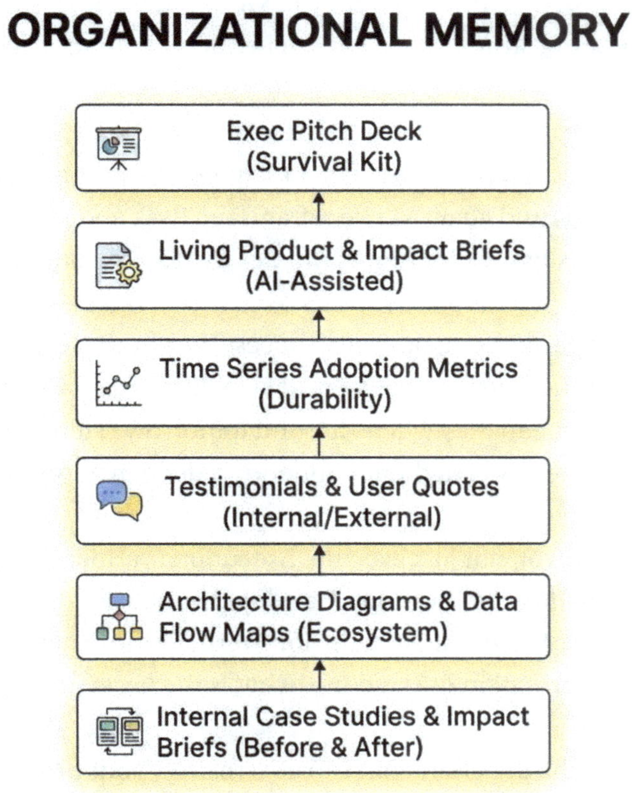

Figure 9-3. *Organizational Memory Checklist*

Normalize the Chaos

Change is not a detour. It is the road. If you choose to work in enterprise, you are choosing a world where turnover, ambiguity, shifting priorities, and reorgs are part of the landscape. Pretending otherwise just makes you more frustrated.

Your job as a product leader is not only to build a good product. It is to build an adaptable system around that product. That includes the people, processes, and stories that keep it moving forward when the environment changes.

Make plans, but hold them loosely. Roadmaps are not contracts with the universe. They are your best guess, informed by what you know today. Build in room to swap, cut, or reorder when a new org structure changes dependencies or priorities. If your plan cannot flex, it will snap.

Design for resilience, not perfection. A perfect plan that only works in a stable org lives for about six weeks. A resilient plan anticipates that teams will be realigned, stakeholders will change, and goals will be reframed. Think about how your product can still deliver value under slightly different mandates instead of optimizing for one exact org shape.

Assume nothing is permanent, not even success. Just because your product is a priority this year does not mean it will be next year. Just because you have a great sponsor today does not mean they will be around tomorrow. Treat every quarter of stability as borrowed time to strengthen foundations, deepen adoption, and harden your value story.

Train your team to pivot, not just execute. Execution is critical, but rigid execution in a changing environment leads to burnout. Develop the muscles of reframing, rescoping, and resequencing without losing sight of the long term vision. Encourage your team to ask, "Given this new information or structure, what is the best next move for our users and our product?"

You cannot control the org chart. You can control how your product adapts to it. You can control how you respond when the change note hits your inbox, how you show up in the first meeting with a new leader, and how calmly you help your team process uncertainty.

Placeholder for Diagram: Circle of control for product leaders during reorgs

A simple tool stack recommendation for this chapter, so you can actually survive org change:

1. **For Capturing Decisions and Creating Durable Artifacts**: Confluence or Notion as the home base, plus a consistent monthly one-pager in Google Docs and a lightweight exec deck in Google Slides.

2. **For Meeting Capture and Fast Synthesis**: An AI meeting notes tool like Zoom AI Companion, Teams recap, Otter, or Fireflies to collect verbatims and decisions, then an AI assistant to turn those into clean summaries and action items.

3. **For Stakeholder Mapping and Coalition Building**: FigJam, Miro, or Mural for influence maps and dependency maps and their AI clustering features to turn scattered input into themes and risks.

4. **For Intake and Visibility During Reorg Churn**: Jira or Asana to track commitments, plus a simple risk register that is visible and updated.

5. **For Communication and Narrative Distribution**: Slack or Teams plus a repeatable update format that AI can help you draft and keep consistent. The goal is not more process. The goal is durable clarity when everything else is moving.

In the next chapter, we will look at how to coach your team through all of this ambiguity in a way that does not just keep them afloat, but actually makes them stronger. We will talk about how to turn uncertainty into agency and complexity into clarity so your team can keep building even when the ground underneath them is shifting.

CHAPTER 10

Coaching Product Teams Through Ambiguity

You do not need a coach when everything is going smoothly. You need one when the roadmap just changed for the third time, leadership is still rewriting the strategy doc, and your team is staring at you like you are supposed to know what to do next.

The point of coaching is not to be the smartest person in the room or to have the most opinions on every decision. It is to help other people become confident in making their own.

Coaching in products is not cheerleading. It is about equipping people with tools, patterns, and instincts so they can operate effectively when context is sparse and the stakes are high. It is about building judgment. Especially when the answers are not obvious and the ground is shifting under your feet.

© Anusha Ravi and Nitika Malhotra 2026
A. Ravi and N. Malhotra, *Launching Enterprise Products*, https://doi.org/10.1007/979-8-8688-2661-0_10

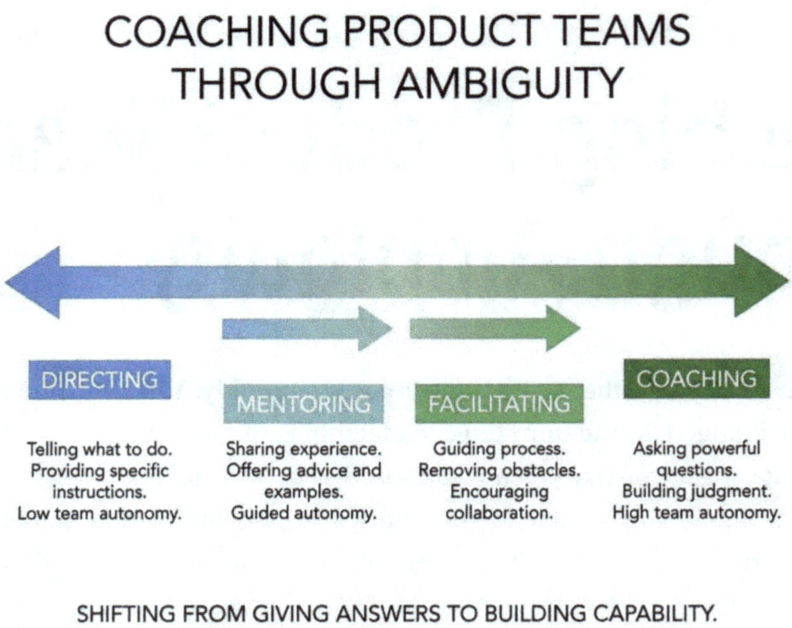

Figure 10-1. *Coaching Spectrum*

Start with Psychological Safety

Coaching through ambiguity starts with creating an environment where people are not afraid to look stupid, be wrong, or change their minds. Very much like raising a toddler, how you respond when someone falls matters more than how often they fall. The way you coach your team around ambiguity becomes the emotional and psychological scaffolding that lets them operate with courage instead of paralysis.

You normalize uncertainty out loud. You say things like, “We do not have all the answers yet” and “Some of this will change as we learn more.” You make it clear that not knowing is acceptable and that asking questions is not a sign of weakness. In fact, it is part of the job.

You reward learning, not just outcomes. When someone runs a sharp experiment, frames a clean hypothesis, or does a solid discovery sprint that disproves a popular idea, you applaud the work, even if the result is "this will not work." You separate the quality of thinking from the luck of the outcome.

You protect calculated risk takers. If someone takes a thoughtful bet and documents the tradeoffs, and it still goes sideways, you defend them in leadership rooms. Your reaction in those moments sets the tone for everyone watching. If risk is punished, your team will default to safe, incremental choices and wait for you to tell them what to do.

You also model vulnerability. When you misjudge something, say so. When you change your mind because new information came in, say that too. When you do not know, say, x"I do not know yet; here is how we will find out." It gives others permission to do the same.

The goal is not comfort. It is confidence. Confidence that failure is not fatal. That progress matters more than perfection. That the team will fall forward together.

In one internal platform team at a large SaaS company, the PM made a point of starting retros with, "Here is one thing I misjudged this quarter." The engineers followed. Designers followed. Over time, ambiguity stopped feeling like a test of personal worth and started feeling like a shared problem to work through. That is psychological safety in action.

Teach Them to Navigate Fog, Not Wait for Clarity

In ambiguous environments, waiting for perfect information is just a slower way of saying no. If your team believes they can only move when everything is known, you will stall on every important decision. Your job is to teach them how to make decisions with just enough information, not all of it.

You coach them to force prioritization. When everything feels blurry, you ask, "What is the riskiest assumption in front of us?" and "What decision, if made, would unblock the most people?" You push them to identify the one or two questions that matter most instead of spinning on twenty smaller ones.

You use time-boxed discovery. You do not let research or exploration expand endlessly. You say, "Take two weeks to test this hypothesis. Talk to five customers. Ship a small experiment. At the end, we will either commit, pivot, or kill the idea." Time boxes give ambiguity edges.

You encourage judgment calls. You explicitly tell the team that decisions do not need unanimous consensus to move forward. You remind them that directional bets, grounded in the best information available, are better than no bets at all. You give them phrases like, "Given what we know today, the best next step is..." so they can act without pretending they are omniscient.

You set decision-making heuristics. You align on principles like "customer impact over internal preference," "truth over comfort," and "velocity over perfection when the blast radius is small." You use these as shared rules of thumb when the path is murky. When a senior leader asks why a call was made, you can point back to the principles, not just personal preference.

You are coaching decisiveness, not recklessness. You want the confidence to act, paired with the humility to adjust when new information arrives.

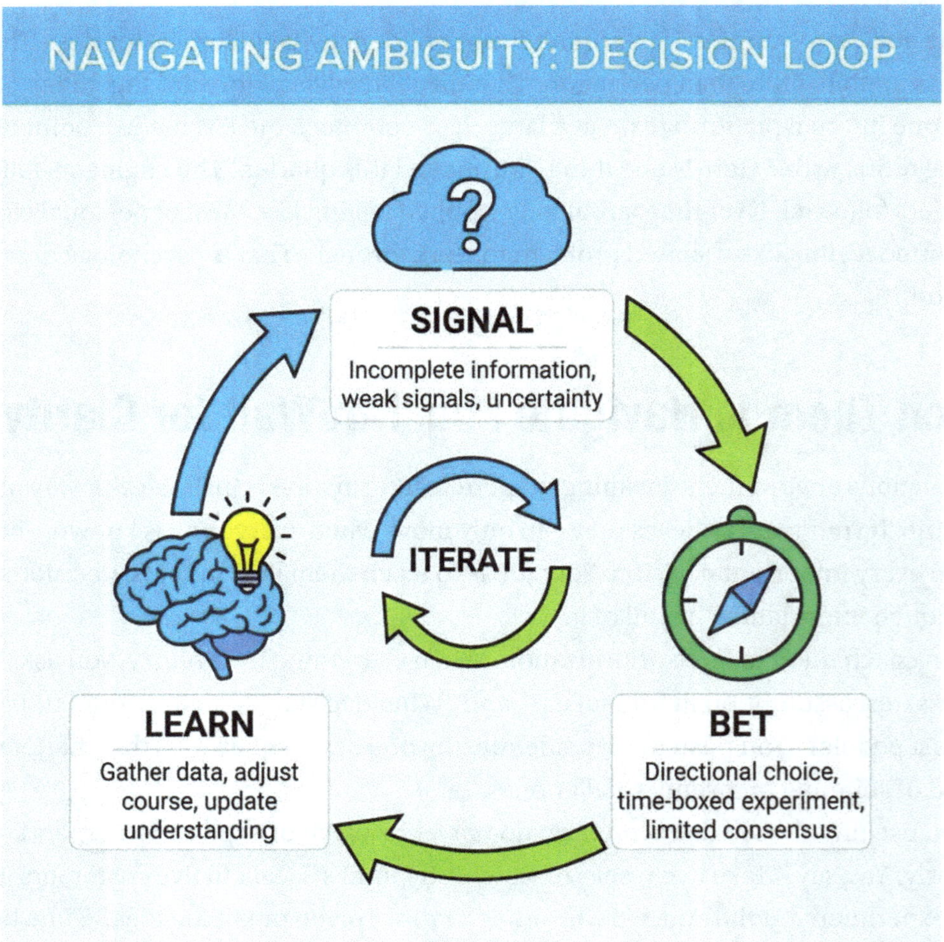

Figure 10-2. *Navigating Ambiguity Decision Loop*

In many platform teams, you see this play out around migration decisions. The team never has perfect information on every edge case before starting a move from system A to system B. The leaders who coach well teach their teams to identify the highest risk flows, plan a phased cutover, and move with a sequence of small, reversible steps. They do not wait three years for the mythical perfect plan that never arrives.

Build Their Strategic Muscle

Your team cannot grow if you are always the one connecting the dots, translating every request into strategy, and holding the entire context in your head. Coaching through ambiguity means teaching people to zoom out and think in bets, not tasks.

You make them own the "why." Before you let someone dive into solution space, you ask them to articulate why the problem matters at all. Who is affected? What changes if we get this right? What breaks if we do nothing? If they cannot explain the strategic importance in simple language, they are not ready to choose a solution.

You ask second-order questions. You sit in one-on-ones and ask, "If this works, what happens next?" and "What does success here unlock for customers or for the business?" You nudge them to think about downstream impact instead of just the ticket in front of them. Over time, they start anticipating those questions and baking that thought process into their own planning.

You expose them to upstream and downstream impact. You do not isolate PMs or leads in the build phase and then hide them from what happens after launch. You bring them into customer calls, ops reviews, post-incident reviews, and quarterly business reviews. You let them see how inputs and outputs connect across functions. That is how product thinkers turn into strategic operators.

You give them visibility into leadership tradeoffs. When roadmaps shift or priorities change, you explain the tradeoffs, not just the decision. You show them the constraints, the pressures, the competing goals that shaped the call. You demystify the machinery. The more they see how decisions are made, the more equipped they are to make their own when you are not in the room.

You are not just coaching for execution. You are developing future heads of product. Start early.

In one enterprise data team, the senior PM made it a rule that any PM who shipped a major capability had to present it in an executive forum, including the "why now" and "what this unlocks next." It was uncomfortable the first few times. Within a year, the entire bench of PMs was more strategic, because they had been forced to practice that muscle repeatedly under real pressure.

Protect Space for Deep Work

Ambiguity often breeds urgency. Urgency, if unmanaged, kills depth. When everything feels unclear, leaders tend to schedule more meetings, spin up more status updates, and ask for more decks. Your team ends up context switching constantly instead of doing the deep thinking required to resolve the ambiguity.

Coaching here means protecting space with intent.

You push back on noisy stakeholders when needed. You say, "If we keep pivoting every three days based on new opinions, we will never get through discovery or commit to a path." You absorb some of the chaos so your team can stay focused on the right problems.

You declare focus periods. Maybe it is a week where you dramatically cut meetings, reduce Slack chatter, and set the expectation that this time is for research, design, and architecture, not status reporting. Focus does not have to be permanent to be powerful.

You limit chaos by structuring time. You can create clear zones for exploration and zones for execution. Mornings for deep work, afternoons for collaboration. First half of the sprint for discovery, second half for delivery. Whatever fits your context, but not everything piled on top of everything else.

You celebrate depth publicly. When someone goes deep into a problem space, unblocks a gnarly dependency, or produces a thoughtful strategy document that clarifies direction, you shine a light on it. You are teaching the team that serious thinking is valued, not just shipping tickets at high speed.

In chaotic environments, focus is a gift. Give it to your team.

You can see the opposite in some internal tool teams where priorities change weekly. PMs are chasing every new request, engineers live in Slack, and nobody gets two uninterrupted hours to think. Those teams do not magically "handle ambiguity better." They just drown in it. The coaching move is to slow the noise down enough that the right work can actually happen.

Coach the Individual, Not Just the Role

Different people react to ambiguity in different ways. Some freeze. Some flail. Some sprint into the fog at full speed and then trip over everything. Coaching is not generic. It is specific to the person in front of you.

You map personalities to environments. You pay attention to who needs more structure and clear boundaries to function well. You notice who thrives with stretch and who needs a bit more runway before you yank away their guardrails. You notice who keeps saying yes to everything and then quietly burns out.

You give direct, compassionate feedback. When someone is avoiding decisions, you say it clearly. When someone is stirring confusion instead of resolving it, you call that out too. You do it in a way that is grounded in care and growth, not blame. "Here is what I am seeing. Here is why it matters. Here is how I want to support you in changing it."

You use stretch assignments wisely. You give people projects that are slightly beyond their current comfort zone, where ambiguity is present but not overwhelming. You do not drop a new PM into a mission-critical, cross-company transformation as their first ambiguous assignment and then get surprised when they struggle. You dial the difficulty up slowly.

You create safety nets. You clarify where and when you will catch them if they fall. You say, "Take the first pass on this, and I will review before it goes to the VP" or "Run this stakeholder conversation, and I will be in the room to back you up." People take smarter risks when they know they are not alone.

People rarely remember the exact feedback you gave them word for word. They do remember how you made them feel when things were uncertain. Supported or alone. Trusted or second-guessed. That emotional memory will shape how they behave the next time ambiguity shows up.

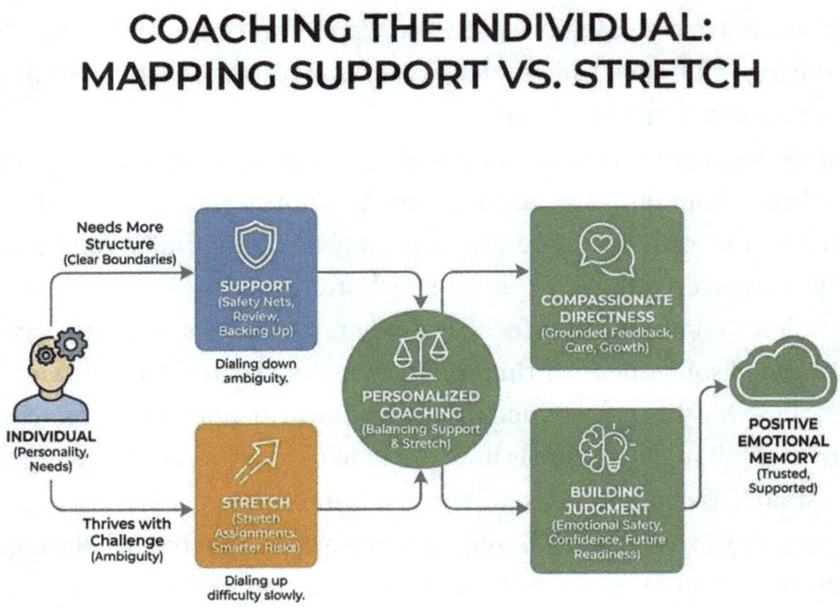

Figure 10-3. *Coaching the Individual*

Measure What Matters

In ambiguous environments, output can feel fuzzy. Everyone is working hard, but nobody is quite sure if they are getting better at handling the ambiguity itself. You can create clarity through a few simple signals.

Instead of only staring at throughput or story points, look at decision velocity. How long does it take from "we see a problem" to "we made a call"? Look at how many hypotheses the team tests in a sprint or a month. Look at the time from insight to iteration. Look at whether the list of open questions is shrinking as work progresses or just changing shape.

You do not need a fancy dashboard for this. A whiteboard with a few tracked decisions and experiments can be enough. The point is to pay attention.

These are not just productivity metrics. They are indicators of a team growing in confidence and competence. A team that used to spend three weeks debating a direction and now lands it in five days with a clear experiment attached is getting stronger, even if the external environment is just as messy as before.

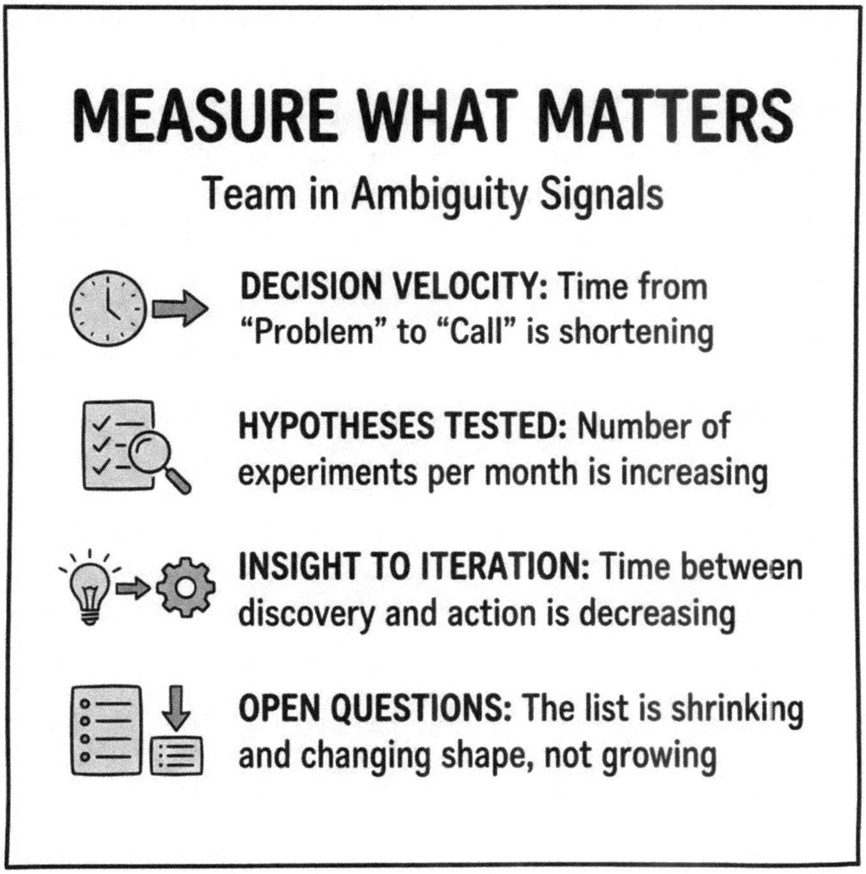

Figure 10-4. *Measure What Matters*

Coaching as Legacy

You will not always be the one steering the ship. At some point you will move teams, change companies, or step into a different scope. What you leave behind will not just be a set of shipped features or a platform diagram. It will be how your team thinks, decides, and behaves when you are not there.

If you coach well through ambiguity, you leave behind people who can hold their own in complex environments. You leave behind a team that is resilient, a product that is more robust, and a culture that is a little more thoughtful and a little less reactive. That is your real legacy.

In the next chapter, we will step back and look at how platform thinking and ecosystems shape these teams and products over time. We will connect the individual coaching you do here with the way products grow from 0 to 1 to n ecosystems, unlocking scale far beyond their original intent.

CHAPTER 11

Platform Thinking and Ecosystems

Most 0 to 1 products begin with a simple, tightly scoped objective. You solve a problem. You unblock a workflow. You automate something repetitive. You launch a feature that makes life easier for one team or a few customers. But the products that eventually transform an organization do not remain confined to that first use case. They grow. They expand. They mature into platforms. And when they become platforms, they stop being a tool. They become the foundation that enables everything else to scale.

The shift from product to platform is not automatic. It requires intention, design, and capability. Many teams try to jump into platform mode too early and collapse into architectural debt. Others get stuck in feature-land and never unlock the broader value their product could have delivered. Platform thinking is the art of knowing when to widen the aperture and how to do it without blowing up what worked in version one.

Knowing the Inflection Point

Not every product should evolve into a platform. But you start noticing signals when the demand around the product begins to shift. For example, you might see multiple teams solving the same problem independently using workarounds on top of your product. Or different business units building custom scripts to tie your tool into their reporting chain. You also notice that your roadmap starts filling with feature requests that are not specific enhancements but structural asks. Things like custom data models, shared provisioning, tenant-aware workflows, or external API access.

This is the inflection point. The product has outgrown being a feature and is now getting pulled into platform territory.

© Anusha Ravi and Nitika Malhotra 2026
A. Ravi and N. Malhotra, *Launching Enterprise Products*, https://doi.org/10.1007/979-8-8688-2661-0_11

A simple example is when you launch a workflow automation feature for a single operations team, and suddenly customer support wants similar automation. Sales wants to reuse the decision engine. Finance wants access to the underlying rules. The repeated pull is telling you something: the capability you built is no longer a point solution. It is a primitive that other teams want to build on.

Another example is an internal reporting tool that started as a dashboard for tracking operational KPIs. Over time, other teams begin asking for access to the underlying dataset, custom metrics, drill downs, data exports, and alerting pipelines. What you built as a dashboard now needs to behave like a data platform. If you ignore that evolution, you force everyone around you into shadow systems.

Platform thinking begins when you recognize that what you built is no longer singular. It is foundational.

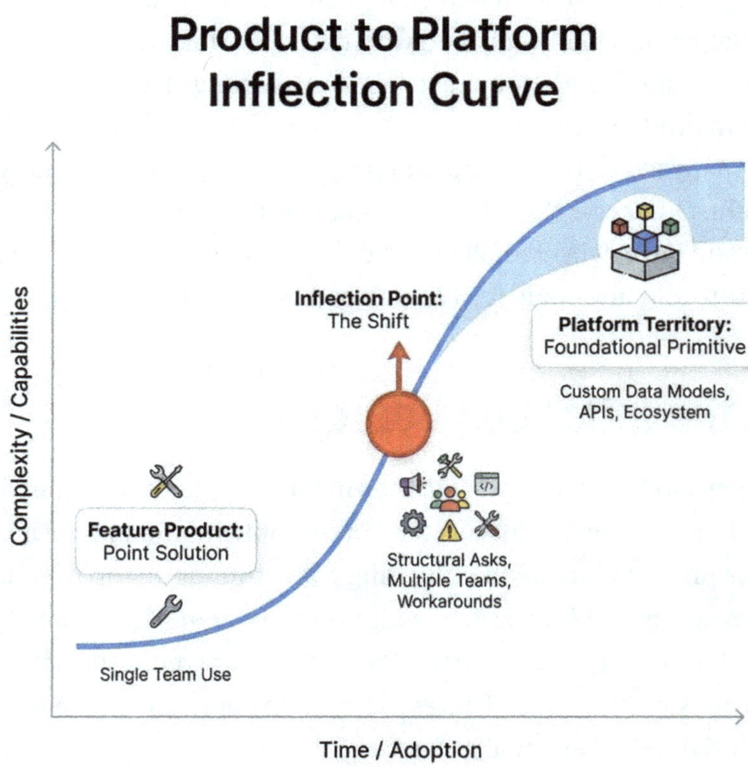

Figure 11-1. *Product-to-Platform Inflection Curve*

How to leverage AI to spot the inflection point before it becomes a fire

AI is very good at pattern recognition across messy inputs, which is exactly what the inflection point looks like in real life. Most teams miss it because the signals are scattered. Requests come in through Slack, email, Jira, random hallway conversations, customer success notes, and escalation threads. Use AI to consolidate and cluster those inputs so you can see the real shape of demand. A practical workflow looks like this. Every week, export or copy the last two to four weeks of platform-related asks from Jira, Slack threads, support tickets, and intake forms. Feed that into an AI assistant and ask it to cluster requests into themes like extensibility, access controls, versioning, data exports, integration points, reliability, and developer experience. Then ask it one more question: "Which of these themes is a platform primitive and which is feature surface area." That simple split helps you see whether you are still in feature land or being pulled into platform territory. You can also use AI to detect duplication across teams. If three teams are independently building scripts or connectors, AI can help you summarize what each script does and where the overlap is. That gives you evidence for platform investment. You can walk into leadership and say, "Here are the repeated workarounds, here is the cost, and here is the primitive we should standardize." That is the inflection point argument in a language leaders understand. Tools that make this easier are the ones you already use. Jira or Asana for intake, Slack or Teams for chatter, and an AI assistant for synthesis. If your org uses Productboard or Jira Product Discovery, even better because those tools structure raw requests and make clustering cleaner.

Designing for Extensibility, Not Just Usability

When you expand from product to platform, your design philosophy must shift. You are no longer optimizing only for usability. You are optimizing for extensibility. That means your product must allow multiple teams to build on top of it without breaking its core principles.

The best platforms do not try to solve every problem. They solve the right primitives and make them accessible. They treat interoperability as a first-class requirement. They expose clean interfaces. They document their boundaries. And they think about scale before scale becomes a fire.

For example, imagine you built an AB testing engine for a single product line. It works well. But other teams begin to use it, and their needs diverge. One wants multi-armed bandits. Another wants batch experimentation. Another needs cross-channel tracking.

If the engine were built as a monolith with hard-coded assumptions, it would become brittle. But if it was built with extensibility in mind, teams can plug in custom logic while still relying on the shared foundation.

Another example is a permissions system. A small product might hard code permissions into the application layer. But a platform needs role-based access, team-based access, service accounts, and auditability. If you modularize this early, teams can extend it. If you do not, every new product that depends on you inherits the pain.

Extensibility means you build the socket, not the appliance.

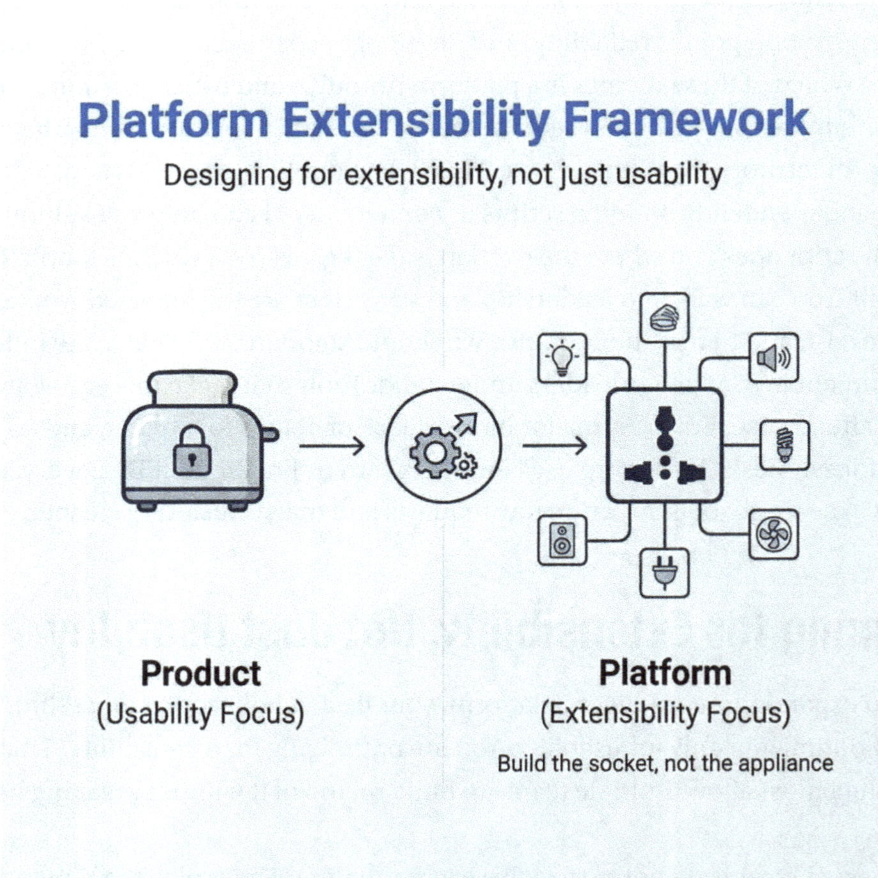

Figure 11-2. *Platform Extensibility Framework*

How to leverage AI to design for extensibility without overbuilding

The risk with platform thinking is that teams either underdesign and create chaos later or overdesign and create a platform that nobody can ship on. AI helps you find the right middle by turning extensibility into a small set of reusable primitives and contracts.

Start with interface clarity. Take your current use cases and the top future asks, and use AI to extract the smallest set of primitives that appear repeatedly. Things like rules, triggers, workflows, identities, permissions, schemas, events, connectors, and policies. Then ask the AI assistant to propose an interface boundary for each one. What belongs in the core? What belongs in extensions? What should configuration be? What must be code? This is the "socket vs. appliance" decision in concrete form. Use AI to pressure test your extensibility model. Give it your proposed API design or module boundaries and ask, "What are the likely failure modes when five different teams build on this?" You will often surface hidden issues like unclear versioning, overly specific assumptions baked into field names, missing audit hooks, or permission edge cases. Those are expensive to fix after adoption scales. Use AI to accelerate documentation and developer experience. Platforms live or die by how fast other teams can build on them. Use AI to draft API docs, example payloads, sample integrations, and starter templates. Then have engineers review for correctness. This is not about perfect docs. It is about removing friction for new builders. Tool wise, this usually maps to an API management and documentation stack. Swagger or OpenAPI for specs, Postman for collections, an API gateway like Apigee or Kong for policy and versioning, and a docs portal like GitBook, Docusaurus, or ReadMe. AI is the glue that turns these from "we have tools" into "people can actually use this."

Treating Your Users Like Partners, Not Consumers

A platform changes the relationship you have with your users. Instead of building for them, you begin building with them. They become co-creators. They rely on your platform for their own roadmaps. Their success depends on your reliability. Their asks become cross-dependent. This is where partnership replaces conventional product management.

You must give users clear contribution paths. For instance, a design system thrives when design and engineering teams can propose new components, patterns, or guidelines. A data platform grows when analytics teams can contribute new models or datasets. An automation platform expands when operations teams propose reusable templates or triggers.

One example from enterprise SaaS is the evolution of internal integration hubs. The core product team builds the connectors and orchestration layer, but other teams create their own connectors because their workflows demand customization.

Instead of fighting that, the smart platform team creates a contribution model. They establish review guidelines, compatibility checks, and versioning expectations. This allows the ecosystem to grow without chaos.

Another example is a centralized ML feature store. The platform team might manage the core storage, lineage, and governance, while individual ML teams contribute features for their specific models. The platform succeeds only when the contributors can operate without breaking the core.

A platform is not a standalone product. It is an ecosystem. And ecosystems require healthy, empowered participants.

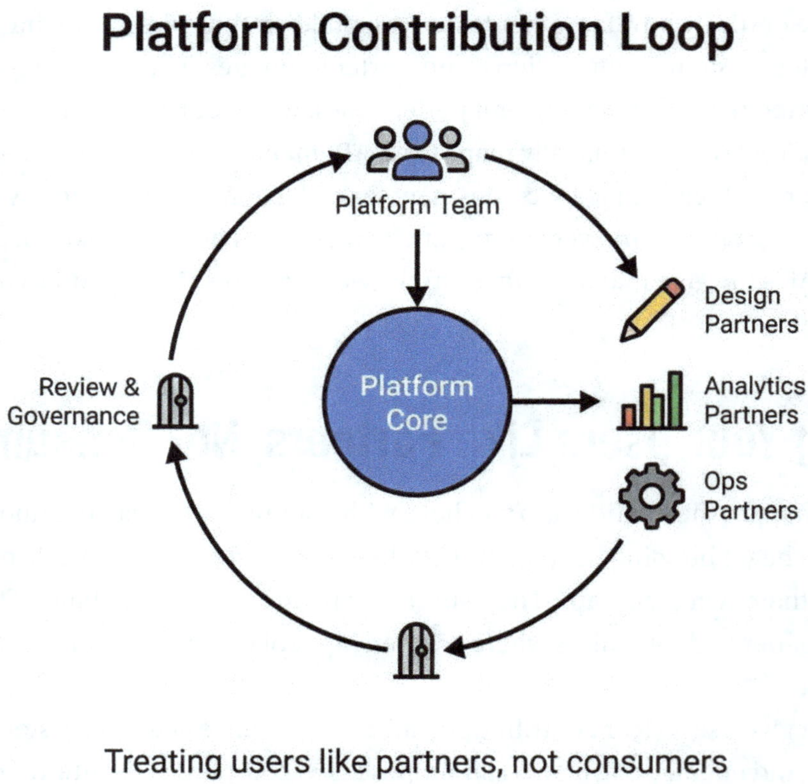

Figure 11-3. *Platform Contribution Loop*

How to leverage AI to build a healthy contribution model and reduce ecosystem chaos

AI helps you scale partnership without drowning in coordination. The first problem platforms hit is not technical. It is contribution friction. People want to extend the platform, but they do not know how, and the core team cannot review everything manually. AI helps you create repeatable contribution paths with clear guardrails. Start by creating contribution templates. Use AI to draft standardized templates for new connectors, new workflow templates, new datasets, or new UI components. Each template should force the contributor to answer the questions that protect the ecosystem: purpose, users, dependencies, data sensitivity, performance considerations, backwards compatibility, observability hooks, and a rollback plan. This turns contribution into a structured process instead of a random PR. Use AI as a first-pass reviewer. Before a contribution even reaches the core team, AI can summarize what changed, detect potential breaking changes, flag missing documentation, and identify policy violations like missing audit logs or missing permission checks. You still need human review, but AI reduces the load and makes reviews faster and more consistent. Then use AI to help you run partner councils.

A platform council usually generates lots of input and very little synthesis. Use AI to summarize council notes into decisions, open questions, and next actions. Publish it in a predictable place. Consistent artifacts make contributors feel respected and keep the ecosystem aligned. Tool-wise, this is where GitHub or GitLab becomes central for contribution workflows, with CODEOWNERS and automated checks. Pair that with a docs home in Confluence, Notion, or a public style docs portal. For design systems, Figma plus a contribution guideline and versioning approach matters more than anything. For data platforms, dbt plus governance and lineage tools become the scaffold. AI sits across all of this and makes the process scalable.

Solving for the Network, Not the Node

When you build a platform, the unit you optimize for is no longer your product. It is the entire ecosystem. You think horizontally, not vertically. You begin to see how different tools, workflows, and teams interact. The goal becomes reducing organizational entropy.

For instance, you standardize core primitives. This might mean agreeing on a consistent definition of customer across all teams. Or standardizing event schemas. Or unifying authentication flows. When you unify these primitives, every product that plugs into the platform inherits stability.

Another example is enabling composition. Instead of building rigid interfaces, you create modular blocks that other teams can combine. This is how API gateways, workflow builders, or notification systems evolve. Teams stitch together capabilities to create their own workflows, while the platform ensures coherence.

The opposite happens when platforms drift. If you allow each extension to modify the core behavior, you end up with incompatible variations. This creates fragmentation. The platform team's job is to prevent drift and maintain cohesion.

A real-world example is an enterprise analytics ecosystem where each team builds its own dashboard tool. Soon enough, the company ends up with twelve BI tools, fragmented metrics definitions, and inconsistent data pipelines. The platform approach consolidates the primitives, defines a single source of truth, and then allows teams to extend strategically.

Network thinking means you stop thinking of your product in isolation. You start thinking of how it fits into the larger enterprise fabric.

How to leverage AI to reduce ecosystem entropy and prevent platform drift

AI helps you see drift earlier than humans can, because drift shows up as small inconsistencies across many artifacts. Different teams name the same event differently. Two groups define "active customer" differently. Three products create slightly different permission models. Over time, those inconsistencies become fragmentation. Use AI to enforce common language. Build a shared glossary for key entities like customer, account, subscription, workflow, experiment, and incident. Then use AI to scan docs, dashboards, and instrumentation names to detect divergence. When it flags that "customer_id" is being used in three different meanings, you have an early warning signal.

Use AI to standardize schemas and contracts. If you have event tracking or data pipelines, AI can review proposed schema changes and warn about downstream break risk. It can also generate migration notes and compatibility guidance. This is especially valuable when multiple teams ship changes in parallel and nobody has full context. Tools that matter here depend on the ecosystem. For data ecosystems, lineage and modeling tools like dbt, DataHub, or Collibra can help maintain standards. For event ecosystems, tools like Segment or RudderStack help standardize event collection. For API ecosystems, an API gateway and OpenAPI specs are the contract layer. AI is what helps you keep the contract clean across many teams.

Building Organizational Infrastructure

A platform is not just a technical construct. It is an organizational construct. You need people, roles, rituals, and accountability models that support the platform's growth. Otherwise, it collapses under its own weight.

This often looks like building a platform product team whose primary job is enablement and governance. Or a developer success team that handles onboarding, troubleshooting, and education. Or a design council that stewards a design system. Or a data governance group that ensures consistency in modeling and access patterns.

For example, imagine a design system that started as a set of Figma components. If it gains adoption, you need versioning guidelines, contribution rules, review cycles, and documentation. Without this scaffolding, the system fragments.

Another example is a workflow automation platform used across multiple business units. Initially, you can support everyone manually. But as adoption scales, you need support processes, office hours, best practice guidelines, escalation paths, and a roadmap council that manages competing priorities.

How to leverage AI to scale the org scaffolding around the platform: AI is your force multiplier for enablement

Platforms scale only when the surrounding organization scales with them. A platform team usually becomes a bottleneck because everyone asks the same questions in different ways. Use AI to build a self-serve knowledge system that actually answers those questions. This includes a searchable FAQ, onboarding guides by persona, troubleshooting runbooks, and example reference implementations. A practical approach is to create a "platform assistant" workflow. Funnel questions from Slack or Teams into a knowledge base. Use AI to suggest answers from existing docs. When the answer is missing, capture the question, write the doc once, and let the assistant serve it next time. Over time, support load drops and consistency increases.

AI also helps with governance operations. For example, if you run office hours, AI can summarize what came up, categorize questions into recurring themes, and propose which docs or features need improvement. If you run a roadmap council, AI can convert noisy debates into clean decisions and recorded rationale. That is organizational infrastructure. Tools that work well here are Confluence or Notion for the knowledge base, Slack or Teams for distribution, Jira for intake and prioritization, and a reliable meeting recap tool like Teams recap, Zoom AI Companion, Otter, or Fireflies for capturing decisions. The exact tool does not matter as much as the loop: capture, synthesize, publish, repeat.

Knowing When to Say No

The hardest part of platform leadership is saying no. A platform's power lies in clarity. If you try to solve every problem, you dilute the core. Not every team's ask belongs inside the platform. Not every integration is a good integration. Not every customization is worth supporting long-term.

You must define the platform's charter clearly. You must articulate what the platform solves and what is out of scope. You must review new requests through the lens of repeatability, leverage, and long-term value. If an ask benefits only one team and adds complexity for everyone else, it does not belong in the core.

A good example is a feature request that demands a highly specific data transformation relevant to only one line of business. If you add it to the platform, you increase maintenance load without increasing ecosystem value. Instead, you create an extension point and let that team build it outside the core.

No is not rejection. No is protection.

How to leverage AI to say no consistently and protect the platform without drama

AI helps you keep your "no" consistent across stakeholders. The main failure mode in platforms is inconsistent exceptions. One exception becomes two, and soon the platform is a junk drawer. Use AI to draft refusal responses that always tie back to the charter, explain the tradeoff, and propose an alternative path like an extension point, a plugin, or a local implementation. AI can also help score requests quickly. Feed it a request and ask it to score on repeatability, ecosystem leverage, long-term maintenance cost, risk, and alignment to platform primitives. You still make the call, but you avoid being purely reactive. Over time, people learn the rules, and you get fewer low-quality requests. Tools here are your intake system, Jira Product Discovery, or Productboard if you have them, plus a visible charter doc. AI makes the response faster, but the charter is what keeps it fair.

Recognizing When the Platform Is Working

A platform is succeeding when adoption happens without friction. When new teams onboard themselves without heavy documentation. When extensions behave predictably. When governance feels natural, not bureaucratic. When the roadmap begins to focus on long-term leverage instead of urgent patchwork.

You know your platform is scaling when you see signals such as teams building on your APIs instead of on top of your UI, or when support tickets shift from "How do I use this" to "How do I optimize this," or when leadership pulls you into strategic planning conversations because your platform is now considered an enabler of future growth.

How to leverage AI to measure ecosystem health and tell the platform story: AI helps you measure the right success signals without drowning in dashboards

Platforms have multiple user types and multiple forms of value. A simple "active users" metric is not enough. Use AI to summarize ecosystem health across four dimensions: adoption, extensibility, reliability, and contribution. For adoption, track onboarding completion, time to first value, and retention for builders and consumers separately. AI can help you segment and interpret these patterns and generate a monthly narrative that leadership can understand. For extensibility, track API usage growth, number of integrations, number of templates or plugins created, and reuse rate. AI can help you identify which primitives are most reused and which ones cause friction or confusion. For reliability, track SLO adherence, incident rate, mean time to detect, and mean time to recover. AI can help you summarize incidents into themes and identify repeat offenders that indicate architectural debt. For contributions, track the number of contributors, PR throughput, review cycle time, and doc coverage. AI can flag where contribution is slowing due to unclear guidelines or missing tooling. Tools that support this usually include Amplitude or Mixpanel for adoption and behavior, Datadog or New Relic for reliability, GitHub or GitLab for contribution metrics, and a docs home base like Confluence, Notion, or GitBook. AI connects these into one coherent story so the platform narrative becomes durable and repeatable.

You stop being a product. You become infrastructure.

Summary

The evolution from product to platform is not accidental. It requires recognizing the inflection point, designing for extensibility, empowering your users as partners, solving for the network instead of the individual, building the organizational scaffolding that sustains growth, knowing when to say no, and learning to measure success by the ecosystem, not by the feature list.

When done well, your product becomes more than a tool. It becomes the foundation the organization builds upon. It becomes leverage. And eventually, it becomes a legacy.

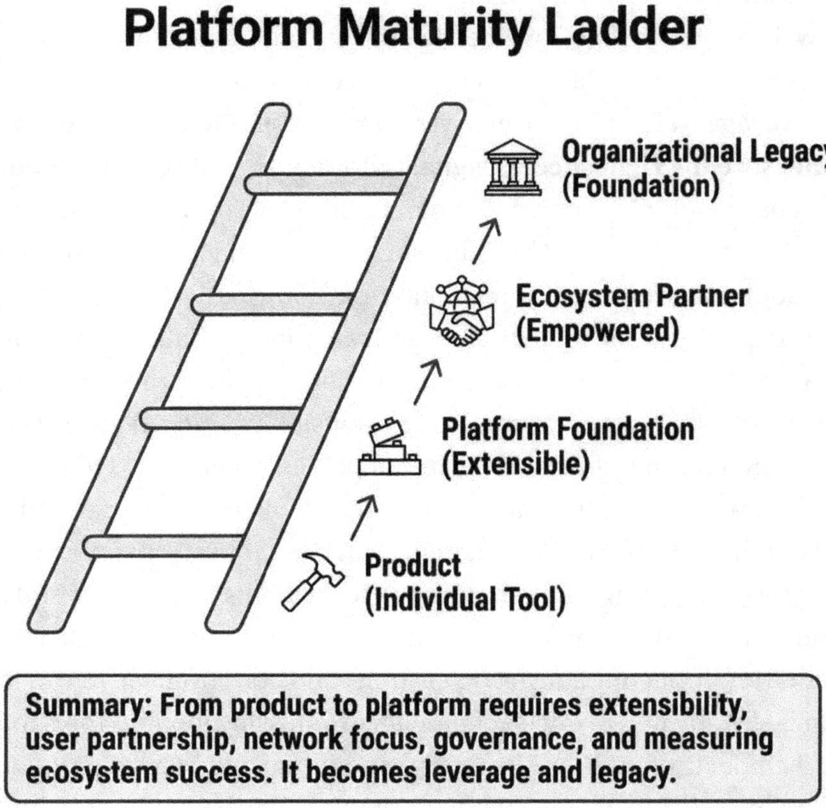

Figure 11-4. *Platform Maturity Ladder*

CHAPTER 12

It's a Wrap! Lessons from the 0 to 1 Journey

The journey from zero to one in enterprise product building is rarely glamorous. It is not a montage of whiteboarding sessions, visionary speeches, or dramatic unveilings. Most of the time, it is a mix of partial information, competing priorities, stubborn systems, and the constant work of creating clarity where none exists. But if you commit to the process, if you stay curious and resilient, and if you learn to read the organization as much as the customer, the journey becomes incredibly rewarding.

This chapter pulls together the mindset, patterns, and behaviors that shape successful 0 to 1 builders. These are not shortcuts. They are durable truths. They are the things you learn only by doing, failing, rebuilding, and succeeding inside complex, high-stakes environments.

Clarity Beats Certainty

In enterprise environments, you almost never get perfect information. You rarely get green lights that come without caveats. You often launch before everything feels ready. And you usually make strategic decisions without knowing all the variables.

The PMs who thrive are not the ones who wait for certainty. They are the ones who create clarity. Clarity about the problem. Clarity about the decision. Clarity about what is true today and what you need to learn next.

For example, imagine you are launching a new upstream ingestion pipeline. The business wants speed. Engineering wants stability. Data science wants structure. Instead of trying to satisfy everyone, you create clarity by defining the goal for version one: reduce ingestion time by 20 percent while maintaining data quality thresholds. Suddenly the room aligns because you anchored everyone to the same understanding.

© Anusha Ravi and Nitika Malhotra 2026
A. Ravi and N. Malhotra, *Launching Enterprise Products*, https://doi.org/10.1007/979-8-8688-2661-0_12

Another example is when leadership debates whether to invest in automation or insights. Instead of choosing sides, you anchor the conversation in business need: which one removes the biggest bottleneck today? Clarity moves people forward. Certainty is optional.

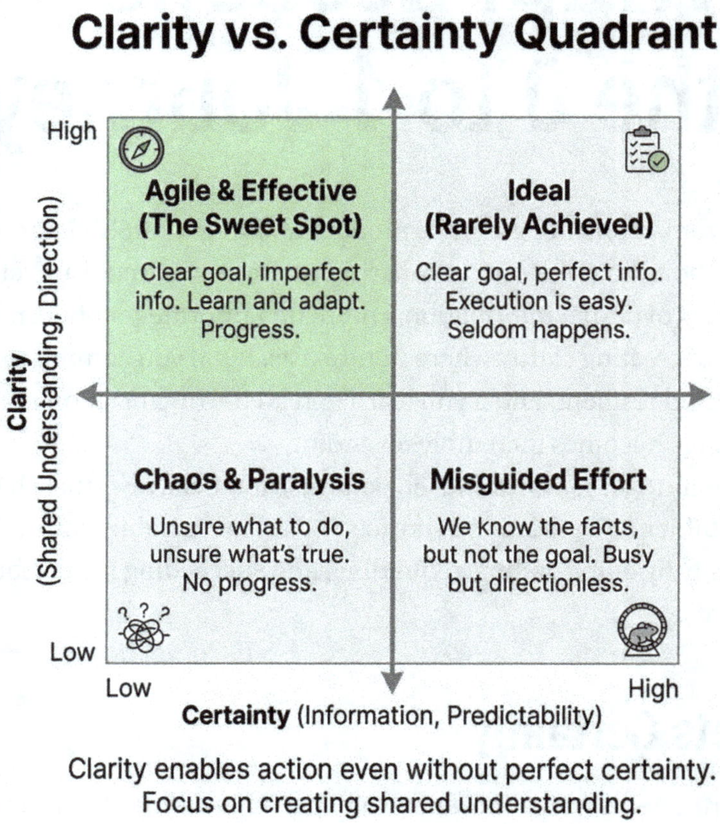

Figure 12-1. *Clarity vs. Certainty Quadrant*

Conviction Is Contagious

If you are not willing to back your product, no one else will. Conviction does not mean stubbornness. It means grounded belief. It means you understand the customer, you trust the problem framing, and you can communicate the value of your solution with confidence.

People follow conviction. They follow the PM who stands in the room and says, "This matters, and here is why." They follow the PM who can articulate the story, the customer pain, the business opportunity, and the long-term value.

For example, think about launching a new experimentation engine in an organization that has never run structured experiments. Many teams will hesitate. Some will say they are not ready. Others will say they do not have time. But if you bring data, examples, and a clear path forward, your conviction becomes the catalyst. Soon enough, teams begin to see what is possible, and the adoption curve accelerates.

Conviction is not arrogance. It is leadership.

Think in Systems, Act in Steps

Enterprise product building requires two opposite muscles. You need to see the system as a whole. But you also need to move in small, deliberate steps. Most failures come from over-indexing on one side. You either zoom too far out and turn strategy into abstraction, or you zoom too far in and lose the bigger context.

For example, imagine launching a customer insights engine. The system view helps you understand how insights power sales, marketing, merchandising, and operations. But the action step is simple: deliver a single insight that saves a team an hour. That small step begins the flywheel.

Or think about platform modernization. The system view recognizes tech debt, scalability issues, and future extensibility. The action step is to migrate one service, restructure one module, or introduce one standardized primitive. That small step compounds.

System thinking tells you where to go. Incremental action gets you there.

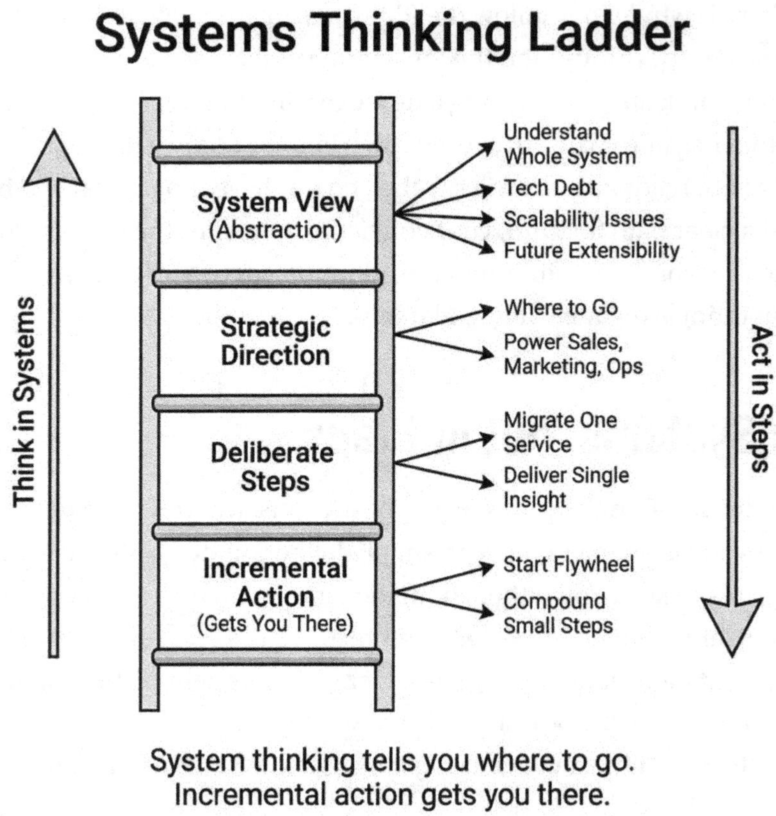

Figure 12-2. *Systems Thinking Ladder*

Scale Trust, Not Just Technology

Technology scales easily. Trust does not. Trust is the currency that lets you launch early. Trust is what lets stakeholders give you autonomy. Trust is what allows teams to move quickly without fear. And trust is built in one decision, one communication, and one follow-through at a time.

For example, imagine shipping a new update to an internal reporting platform. If you previously delivered on time, communicated clearly, and fixed issues quickly, stakeholders give you more runway, even when the next release carries risk. But if earlier releases were chaotic, the trust debt becomes heavy, and every decision becomes harder.

Another example is navigating a major failure. If you own the mistake, share the learnings, and present a clear recovery plan, trust increases. If you deflect or hide information, trust collapses even if the technical problem gets resolved.

The PMs who scale trust are the ones who lead the fastest organizations.

Build Products, But Leave Legacies

The best product builders do not just create features. They shift the way an organization thinks about problems. They inspire teams to adopt better practices. They create frameworks that outlast them. They introduce vocabulary that becomes part of the company culture. They build capabilities that enable entirely new strategies.

For example, if you build a forecasting platform that becomes foundational to demand planning, the feature matters, but the legacy is that you helped the company shift from reactive to predictive decision-making. Or if you build an automated testing framework that becomes the backbone of every launch, the framework is your contribution, but the legacy is that you made quality scalable.

AI in Product World

The product world is in one of those rare transitions where the rules are not fully written yet. For years, enterprise product management was mostly about building workflows, scaling platforms, and negotiating org complexity. That is still true. But now there is a new layer on top: AI is changing what users expect, how fast teams can build, and what "good" even looks like. In the old world, shipping was the hard part. In the new world, it is very possible to ship fast and still be wrong. The craft is shifting from building more to building wisely.

What is changing on the product side is that enterprise software is moving from systems of record to systems of action. The best products are no longer just capturing data. They are doing something with it. They are recommending, prioritizing, predicting, drafting, summarizing, and automating. Users are starting to ask, "Why do I need to click through five screens when the system already knows what I am trying to do?" That expectation is not going away. That is the new bar. What is changing on the AI side is that capability is becoming cheap and ubiquitous. Models are getting better, tooling is more accessible, and prototypes can be built in days. That means differentiation is less about having AI and more about having taste, boundaries, and trust.

In enterprise, "cool" is not the goal. Safe, reliable, explainable, and adoptable is the goal. AI will get you attention. Only product thinking will get you adoption. This is the moment where enterprise PMs can make a massive mark, because enterprises have something most AI startups do not: real workflows, real data, real constraints, and real distribution. If you can layer AI into the right part of an enterprise workflow, you do not just build a feature. You change how work happens. That is leverage. So what does it mean to be a modern enterprise PM in this landscape? It means you become fluent in three new product muscles while keeping the old ones strong.

First, you learn to productize intelligence, not just ship features. The question is no longer "Can we build it." The question is "Where does intelligence remove friction in a way users will trust?" This starts with identifying high-pain, high-repetition, high-cost workflows. The best AI wins are boring. They reduce tickets. They cut cycle time. They eliminate copy paste. They draft the first pass of something humans already do. If your AI idea cannot be tied to a measurable reduction in effort, risk, or delay, it is probably a demo, not a product.

Second, you learn to design for human plus machine collaboration. In enterprise, full automation is rarely the first win. The win is assisted workflows. Draft and review. Suggest and approve. Detect and escalate. Summarize and decide. The PM skill is knowing where the human stays in the loop and what the loop should feel like. That is not an AI problem. That is a product problem. If the AI is wrong sometimes, how does the user recover? If the AI is uncertain, how does it signal that? If a user corrects it, does the system learn, or does it repeat the same mistake forever? These are the adoption breakers, and they are where great PMs differentiate.

Third, you learn to treat trust as a first-class product requirement. AI changes the trust contract. Users will forgive a slow workflow. They will not forgive a workflow that makes up answers, leaks sensitive data, or creates outcomes they cannot explain. In enterprise, the trust stack includes governance, security, audit trails, and clear accountability for errors. It also includes smaller things like permission-aware responses, clear citations to source data, and a predictable user experience where the user understands what the system is doing.

The PM who can navigate trust, compliance, and user value at the same time becomes extremely valuable. Now here is the part that should give you energy. This is not a moment where enterprise PMs get replaced. This is a moment where enterprise PMs who adapt become dangerous in the best way. Because AI makes execution cheaper, and that means judgment becomes the scarce skill. The PM who can frame the right problem, pick the right bet, protect the team from noise, and build adoption loops will outpace the PM who just ships features. So how do you actually make your mark in the next few years?

You focus on four things that compound. One, become the translator between AI capability and business value. Most leaders either overhype AI or fear it. Your job is to stay grounded. You learn what the models can do well, what they cannot do, and where they break. Then you translate that into real use cases, risk boundaries, and a roadmap that is credible. You become the person who can say, "Yes, we can automate this part safely" or "No, this is too sensitive, but we can still reduce effort by doing X." That credibility makes you a leader people trust when everyone else is either panicking or overselling. Two, build the habit of rapid learning loops. AI makes it easy to prototype, which means the best teams will test more. Your advantage will come from how quickly you can run small experiments, learn, and iterate.

The winners will not be the teams with the fanciest model. They will be the teams with the fastest learning loops and the clearest success criteria. You define the leading signal, lagging signal, and sentiment, and you run the loop again and again until it lands. Three, invest in the boring platform foundations that make AI usable. Data quality. Event schemas. Permission models. Observability. Versioning. Evaluation harnesses. Feedback collection. Human override paths. Without these, AI features become unpredictable and fragile, and leadership will lose trust fast. With these, AI becomes a reliable layer that can expand over time. This is where enterprise PMs shine, because you already live in the world of constraints and systems. Four, become a narrative leader. In the AI era, noise will increase.

People will ship prototypes, claim success, show demos, and confuse leadership. Your ability to tell the truth calmly, backed by evidence, will be a differentiator. You do not need to be loud. You need to be clear. You tell the story of what was launched, what was learned, what changed for users, what is still unknown, and what the next bet is. That is how you protect trust and keep momentum. If there is one final meta lesson from the 0 to 1 journey in the age of AI, it is this. Speed is not the advantage anymore. Clarity is. Plenty of teams can move fast now. The teams that win are the ones who can move fast in the right direction with the right guardrails and bring the organization with them. Your mark in this landscape will not come from chasing every new AI wave. It will come from doing what great enterprise PMs have always done, just with higher-leverage tools. You will turn ambiguity into a plan. You will turn noise into signal. You will turn capabilities into outcomes. And you will build things that last long enough to matter.

A legacy is not about personal credit. It is about lasting impact.

Lessons That Stand the Test of Time

When you strip the journey down to its essence, the things that matter most are simple.

Clarity is more important than certainty.

Ambiguity is part of the job. Clarity is what moves people forward. It's what lets you act when not everything is known. As Jason Fried puts it,

> *"A good way to be unsure about something is to ask for one more opinion. More opinions often lead to indecision, not clarity. If necessary, ask for a few, add your own, make a call, and move on."*

Conviction attracts alignment.

You don't need to be the loudest in the room. But you do need to stand behind your product. Stakeholders rally around belief that's grounded in real understanding. Marty Cagan captured this simply:

> *"Great products are engineered when product managers truly understand their customers' problems."*

Small steps compound into systemic change.

The magic is not in the big bang. It's in the quiet, deliberate moves that accumulate over time. Or as Jeff Bezos says,

> *"Be stubborn on vision but flexible on details."*

Trust scales faster than technology.

Tools move fast. Trust moves everything. When people believe in how you work, how you communicate, how you recover, and how you lead, they give you more room to operate. Jim Collins once wrote,

> *"Building a visionary company requires one percent vision and 99 percent alignment."* That alignment is built on trust.

Products come and go. Platforms evolve. But legacies endure.

What you build matters. But how you build it matters even more. That's what people remember. That's what shapes teams and cultures. Or as Jeff Patton said:

> *"At the end of the day, your job isn't to get the requirements right—your job is to change the world."*

These aren't just reflections from thought leaders. They're principles that hold up in the real world, under real pressure, across real orgs. And if you internalize even two of them, you'll be building not just roadmaps but a reputation.

Final Reflection

Enterprise product building is messy, nonlinear, and occasionally chaotic. But it is also deeply fulfilling because you create real change inside real systems that affect real people. You transform workflows. You enable teams. You shape the future of how the business works.

The next chapter is always waiting. The next problem is always around the corner. But with the foundation you now have, you are not starting from zero again. You are starting from experience.

APPENDIX

Chapter Templates (Ready-to-Use)

How to Use This Appendix

1. Find the template for your chapter.
2. Copy/paste into your working doc.
3. Fill it in **as-is** before you start building.
4. Keep each template to **1–2 pages**.

Chapter 1—Problem Behind the Brief

Template

- **Brief request (verbatim):** (copy the exact words you were given)
- **Requester + why now:** (pressure, urgency, deadline, risk)
- **Primary user/persona:** (role + segment)
- **Workflow context:** (where/when the pain occurs)
- **Problem statement (no solution language):**
    - For [user], [pain] happens when [context], causing [impact].
- **Impact today:** (time, cost, risk, quality, satisfaction)
- **Evidence (what we know is true):** (facts, logs, direct observation, quotes)
- **Assumptions (what we need to validate):**

© Anusha Ravi and Nitika Malhotra 2026
A. Ravi and N. Malhotra, *Launching Enterprise Products*, https://doi.org/10.1007/979-8-8688-2661-0

- **Constraints:** (security, compliance, platform, policy, timeline)
- **Success signals:** (outcomes + how you'll measure them)
- **Non-goals:** (explicitly out of scope for now)

Common mistake: Writing a "problem" that is actually a solution (e.g., "we need a dashboard") instead of the user pain and impact.

Chapter 2—Stakeholder Alignment Map

- **When to use:** You need to align people early without letting the work get hijacked.
- **What to fill:** Key stakeholders, what they want/fear, engagement plan, and what you need from them.

Template (Table)

Stakeholder/ Team	Influence (H/M/L)	What they want	What they fear	Can approve/ block what?	Best engagement	What you need from them
-						
-						
-						
-						

Notes (optional)

- **Sponsor (name + role):**
- **Decision forum (where final calls happen):**
- **Update cadence (weekly/biweekly + artifact):**

Common mistake: Treating stakeholders as "audience" instead of "decision makers" (i.e., not clarifying who can actually approve or block).

Chapter 3—V1 Thin Slice Scope

- **When to use:** You're defining V1 and want momentum without boiling the ocean.
- **What to fill:** One scenario, must-haves, non-goals, dependencies, risks, telemetry.

Template

- **North Star outcome (one sentence):** (the user/business change you want)
- **V1 scenario (start → success):**
    - **Start:** (trigger)
    - **Key steps:** (2–4 steps max)
    - **Success moment:** (first value)
- **Must-haves (max 5):**
    1.
    2.
    3.
    4.
    5.
- **Non-goals (explicit):**
- **Dependencies:**
- **Top risks + mitigation:**
    - **Risk:** ___ | **Mitigation:** ___
    - **Risk:** ___ | **Mitigation:** ___
    - **Risk:** ___ | **Mitigation:** ___
- **Telemetry required in V1:**

Common mistake: Calling something "V1" while silently including V3 requirements (especially edge-case perfection and broad configurability).

Chapter 4—Signal vs. Noise Triage

- **When to use:** You have conflicting inputs and need a clean way to prioritize.
- **What to fill:** Each input, credibility, severity, decision, and next step.

Template (Table)

Feedback/ Input	Source	Segment	Specific (H/M/L)	Frequent (H/M/L)	Severe (H/M/L)	Confidence (H/M/L)	Decision (Act/ Investigate/ Park)	Next step
-								
-								
-								
-								

Common mistake: Acting on the loudest feedback instead of the most credible, specific, and high-impact signal.

Chapter 5—Resistance Pre-Wire Plan

- **When to use:** You anticipate internal resistance and need to land a decision cleanly.
- **What to fill:** Blockers, incentives, safety conditions, pre-wire sequence, pilot fallback.

Template

- **Decision needed (precise):**
- **Who can block it (names/teams):**
- **Likely resistance (real reasons):**
- **What would make this safe enough to try (guardrails, pilot, controls):**

- **Pre-wire sequence (order of 1:1s):**
    1.
    2.
    3.
- **Proof to bring:** (data, risks, tradeoffs, precedent)
- **Fallback option (if they say no):**
- **Pilot proposal (smallest safe test):**

Common mistake: Trying to "win" the meeting instead of reducing risk and fear before the meeting.

Chapter 6—Adoption Plan One-Pager

- **When to use:** You're preparing rollout and want adoption built-in, not forced.
- **What to fill:** Target users, activation moment, enablement, support, rollout, metrics, risks.

Template

- **Target users (roles/segments):**
- **Value message (one sentence):**
- **Activation moment (first success):**
- **Onboarding plan:** (in-product/training/champions/defaults)
- **Enablement assets (check what you'll produce):**
    1. ☐ Release note
    2. ☐ 1-page guide
    3. ☐ Demo script
    4. ☐ FAQ/troubleshooting
    5. ☐ Admin/config guide (if needed)

- **Support model:**
- **Rollout plan (pilot → phased → GA):**
- **Adoption metrics:**
    1. **Activation %:**
    2. **Usage depth (key action):**
    3. **Retention (week 4+):**
    4. **Outcome metric:**
- **Top adoption risks + mitigation:**
    1. **Risk: ___ | Mitigation: ___**
    2. **Risk: ___ | Mitigation: ___**

Common mistake: Treating adoption as "comms and training" instead of designing the activation path and defaults inside the product.

Chapter 7—Data Story Memo

- **When to use:** Metrics are unclear or disappointing, and you need an executive-ready narrative.
- **What to fill:** Expectation vs. reality, drivers, what you know/don't know, next actions, and guardrails.

Template (keep to 1 page)

- **What we expected:**
- **What happened (top 1–2 metrics):**
- **Most likely drivers (ranked):**
    1.
    2.
    3.

- **What we know vs. don't know:**
    - **Know:**
    - **Don't know (yet):**
- **Recommendation (what we will do next):**
- **Guardrails (what must not break):**
- **Next check-in date + what we'll measure:**

Common mistake: Dumping charts without naming drivers, uncertainty, and the next decision.

Chapter 8—Platform Capability Canvas

- **When to use:** You're moving from one-off features to scalable platform building.
- **What to fill:** Capability, users, contract, reliability, governance, versioning.

Template (Table)

Capability name	Who uses it?	What it enables	Contract/ interface (API/event/ config)	Reliability needs (SLA/ SLO)	Governance (who approves change)	Versioning and deprecation plan
-						
-						

Notes (optional)

- **Owner (team):**
- **Observability (metrics/logs):**
- **Support model:**

Common mistake: Calling something a "platform" without defining contracts, ownership, and a deprecation path.

Chapter 9—Reorg Reset Memo

- **When to use:** After reorgs, leadership changes, or shifting priorities.
- **What to fill:** What changed, what remains true, decision rights, next milestone, and asks.

Template

- **What changed (facts only):**
- **What remains true (problem/users/value):**
- **What's paused vs. active:**
- **Updated stakeholders + decision rights:**
- **Dependencies that changed:**
- **Next milestone (smallest win in 2–4 weeks):**
- **Risks introduced by the reorg:**
- **Ask (what you need from leadership):**

Common mistake: Restarting from zero instead of preserving what remains true and protecting momentum with a small win.

Chapter 10—Ambiguity → Experiment Planner

- **When to use:** You have uncertainty and need to convert it into learning.
- **What to fill:** Unknowns, hypothesis, smallest test, metrics, timebox, decision rule.

Template (Table)

Biggest unknown	Why it matters	Hypothesis (If X, then Y because Z)	Smallest test	Success metric	Timebox	Decision rule (Ship/Iterate/Stop)	Owner
-							
-							

Common mistake: Treating uncertainty as a discussion topic instead of designing a test with a decision rule.

Chapter 11—Ecosystem Strategy Canvas

- **When to use:** You're designing for extensions, integrations, partners, or internal builders.
- **What to fill:** Builder personas, incentives, distribution, trust, friction reducers, and health metrics.

Template

- **Core platform value (one sentence):**
- **Who builds on it:** (internal teams/partners/customers)
- **Top 3 use cases you want to attract:**
  1.
  2.
  3.
- **Builder incentives (why they invest):**
- **Distribution mechanism:** (marketplace/catalog/internal program)
- **Trust model:** (security review, certification, permissions)
- **Friction reducers:** (sandbox, docs, templates, samples)
- **Ecosystem health metrics:**
  - **Active builders:**
  - **Active extensions/integrations:**

- **Time-to-first-success:**
- **Retention:**

Common mistake: Trying to "grow an ecosystem" without making it low-friction and safe for builders to succeed.

Chapter 12—Post-Launch Review + Lessons Log

- **When to use:** After launch to lock in learning and build repeatable strength.
- **What to fill:** What you aimed to prove, what shipped, real usage, lessons, next plan.

Template

- **What we set out to prove:**
- **What we shipped (scope recap):**
- **What users actually did:**
- **What worked (why):**
- **What didn't (why):**
- **Biggest surprise:**
- **Metrics snapshot (top 3):**

  1.

  2.

  3.

- **Lessons worth reusing next time:**
- **Next plan:**
  - **30 days:**
  - **60 days:**
  - **90 days:**

Common mistake: Moving on after launch without capturing what you learned and how it changes the next iteration.

Glossary

The following is a glossary of terms related to enterprise product management

#	Term	Definition
1	**Adoption**	Sustained, repeat use of a product or feature that results in measurable value.
2	**Affinity Mapping**	Synthesizing raw notes by clustering them into themes to reveal patterns.
3	**API**	Application programming interface; a defined way for systems to communicate.
4	**Backward Compatibility**	Ensuring existing behaviors/integrations keep working after a change.
5	**Business Case**	A justification for investing in a product change, tying cost to expected impact.
6	**Change Management**	Helping people/processes successfully transition to a new way of working.
7	**Champion**	A credible internal advocate who drives awareness, enablement, and momentum.
8	**Churn**	The rate at which usage, users, or customers decline over time.
9	**Constraint**	A non-negotiable limitation (security, compliance, platform, timeline, budget).
10	**Customer Journey**	End-to-end view of how a user experiences a process across touchpoints.
11	**Data Contract**	Agreement on data meaning, ownership, quality, schema, and change rules.
12	**Decision Rights**	Clarity on who decides what (and how disagreements are resolved).
13	**Design Partner**	A trusted early user/customer who co-develops and validates solutions.

(*continued*)

© Anusha Ravi and Nitika Malhotra 2026
A. Ravi and N. Malhotra, *Launching Enterprise Products*, https://doi.org/10.1007/979-8-8688-2661-0

#	Term	Definition
14	**Discovery**	Learning activities that reduce uncertainty about the problem, user, and value.
15	**Dual-Track**	Discovery and delivery running in parallel with continuous feedback loops.
16	**Ecosystem**	Complementary apps, partners, integrations, and extensions around a platform.
17	**Enablement**	Training, docs, comms, and in-product guidance that helps users succeed.
18	**Enterprise**	High-scale environment with complex workflows, many stakeholders, and governance.
19	**Experiment**	A structured test to validate a hypothesis with measurable outcomes.
20	**Feature Flag**	Ability to toggle functionality by segment without redeploying code.
21	**Friction**	Extra effort/time/confusion that blocks users from reaching an outcome.
22	**Governance**	Controls and decision processes that ensure consistency, safety, and compliance.
23	**Guardrails**	Constraints/checks that prevent unsafe, non-compliant, or harmful outcomes.
24	**Hypothesis**	A testable statement linking an intervention to an expected outcome.
25	**Instrumentation**	Tracking/telemetry added to observe behavior and measure outcomes.
26	**Integration**	A connection between systems to exchange data or trigger workflows.
27	**JTBD (Jobs To Be Done)**	Framework describing what users are trying to accomplish and why.
28	**KPI**	Key performance indicator; a measurable signal of progress or health.
29	**Lagging Indicator**	Metric that confirms outcomes after the fact (e.g., revenue).
30	**Leading Indicator**	Metric that moves earlier and predicts outcomes (e.g., activation).
31	**LLM**	Large language model; generates/transforms text (and sometimes other modalities).

(*continued*)

#	Term	Definition
32	**MVP**	Minimum viable product; smallest version that tests core value with real users.
33	**Metrics Tree**	Hierarchy from business objective → product outcomes → leading indicators → events.
34	**North Star Metric**	Primary outcome metric representing the core value delivered.
35	**Non-Goals**	Explicit list of what is out of scope (to protect focus and avoid churn).
36	**OKR**	Objectives and key results; goals paired with measurable results.
37	**Outcome**	User or business impact (behavior change), not the shipped artifact.
38	**Output**	The shipped artifact (feature, UI, workflow, integration).
39	**Platform**	Shared capabilities enabling multiple products/teams to build faster and scale.
40	**Platform Thinking**	Designing for reuse, extensibility, ecosystem growth—not one-off features.
41	**PRD**	Product requirements document; narrative of what/why, constraints, and success criteria.
42	**Problem Statement**	Crisp description of pain and context without prescribing a solution.
43	**Prompt**	Instructions/context given to an AI model to produce a targeted output.
44	**RACI**	Responsibility matrix: responsible, accountable, consulted, informed.
45	**RAG**	Retrieval-augmented generation; model uses retrieved sources as context for accuracy.
46	**Release Train**	Predictable cadence for shipping and coordinating across teams.
47	**Roadmap**	Prioritized plan of outcomes/initiatives over time (with managed uncertainty).
48	**Rollout**	How a feature is introduced (pilot → phased launch → general availability).
49	**Scope**	Boundaries of what will and will not be built in a given iteration.
50	**Signal vs. Noise**	Separating reliable indicators from misleading or low-quality inputs.

(continued)

#	Term	Definition
51	**SLA**	Service-level agreement; uptime/latency/support commitments.
52	**Stakeholder**	Anyone who influences, funds, uses, or is impacted by the product.
53	**Stakeholder Map**	Stakeholders plotted by influence and interest to tailor engagement.
54	**Telemetry**	Event/log/metric data showing real behavior and system performance.
55	**Technical Debt**	Future cost created by shortcuts taken today.
56	**Trade-off**	Deliberate choice where improving one dimension affects another.
57	**Value Realization**	Ensuring shipped capability becomes measurable impact in the real world.
58	**Workflow**	Multi-step user process across roles, policies, and systems.
59	**Zero-to-One**	Building a net-new capability where uncertainty is high and learning is primary.

Index

A

B

© Anusha Ravi and Nitika Malhotra 2026
A. Ravi and N. Malhotra, *Launching Enterprise Products*, https://doi.org/10.1007/979-8-8688-2661-0

C

D

E

L

M

N

O

P, Q

V

W, X, Y

Z

GPSR Compliance
The European Union's (EU) General Product Safety Regulation (GPSR) is a set of rules that requires consumer products to be safe and our obligations to ensure this.

If you have any concerns about our products, you can contact us on

ProductSafety@springernature.com

In case Publisher is established outside the EU, the EU authorized representative is:

Springer Nature Customer Service Center GmbH
Europaplatz 3
69115 Heidelberg, Germany

www.ingramcontent.com/pod-product-compliance
Lightning Source LLC
LaVergne TN
LVHW082340200926
848481LV00012B/3405
9798868826603